I SURVIVED

Stanley W Swain

Stanley Swain.

First published in Great Britain
by Stanley W Swain
The Sheiling
5 Denmark Rise
Diss
Norfolk IP22 3LG
1994

ISBN 0 9523501 0 6

Front cover illustration by John Scriven

Design and artwork by
GetSet, Wortham, Diss IP22 1PX
Set in Garamond Medium
9½ on 10½ point

Printed in England by
Studio Print
23 Charles Wood Road
Rash's Green Industrial Estate
East Dereham
Norfolk NR19 1SX

Contents

ACKNOWLEDGEMENTS

MY thanks are due to many for their help and advice, but in particular I am grateful to Mr H E Tune who introduced my first article to Mr R Russell, editor of the Blue Star Line's house magazine, *Gangway,* who considered it suitable to publish, followed by additional stories. Also to Mr L D Shakespear when he succeeded Mr Russell on his retirement, and thought it worthwhile to include more of my short stories in later editions of *Gangway.* Much encouraged by the reported interest shown in the articles, I decided to combine them, in full, with new material into book form and I am indebted to Mr Derek Palgrave for his advice in this field and also to Mr Brian McDearmid for his help and advice on many subjects.

I was further encouraged when Mr C H Milson, editor of *Sea Breezes* published one of my stories.

I am also indebted to the Blue Star Line management for providing photographs of the ships in which I sailed, and for permission to use them together with more suitable chapter headings for some of the stories, etc. Also to Mrs M Clark and Mr R A Carr who kindly, provided from the archives, the ship photographs.

My thanks also to the Hong Kong Goverment Information Services and the Japan Information and Cultural Centre, for permission to use their photographs; Jeremy Hawes for providing old postcards of Rockhampton, Townsville and Cairns railway.

DEDICATION

TO my wife, Grace, without whose help, patience and encouragement, this book would not have materialised. Also to our daughter, Elaine, who gave her time and typed many of the chapters.

Also to the shipmates I sailed with and to the memory of those who did not survive the War at sea. Hopefully, my small history gives a glimpse of life at sea of the average Merchant Navy man before, during and shortly after the War ended.

In retrospect, I shall always appreciate it was my privilege to have served in the Mercantile Marine. I consider the 12 years at sea taught me some of the real values in life.

FOREWORD

by Vice Admiral Sir Robert Hill, KBE, FEng, FIMarE

Deputy President, the Institute of Marine Engineers
formerly Chief Naval Engineer Officer

STANLEY Swain served as an engineer officer in the Merchant Navy continuously from 1937 to 1949, and the two words of the title of this book express his feelings at having witnessed World War II from engine rooms and boiler rooms of ships of the Blue Star Line.

In his address in Liverpool Cathedral at the service to mark the 50th anniversary of the Battle of the Atlantic The Right Reverend John Hapgood, Bishop of York, said:

> "The Battle of the Atlantic was the longest battle of the war, and in many ways it was the most complex, involving huge deployments over huge distances. . . . At the heart of it were civilians, the men of the Merchant Navy, defenceless targets if naval protection had failed. And what was remarkable about these men was that for voyage after voyage they signed on, again and again, to return to danger. 2000 ships were sunk by submarine in the North Atlantic . . ."

But this is not a war story as such, rather it is a collection of fascinating accounts of events in the life of a marine engineer of those years, with the inherent risks of the profession further heightened by ever-present and unseen threat of explosion and sinking.

There are shipwreck and storms; study and hardship ashore as well as afloat; and two hair-raising accounts of attacks by enraged firemen. But throughout the book runs a great sense of enjoyment of life, and pride and satisfaction at keeping the ordered revolutions and completing the voyage. These are the satisfactions that all marine engineers can recall and share.

He does not dwell on the technology, but his tales instantly evoke the sound and smell of the engine and boiler rooms, and will reawaken many people's own memories.

The Institute of Marine Engineers is privileged indeed to further the marine engineering profession and to represent people who, like Stanley Swain, have made such an enormous contribution to the wealth and freedom of this country, and to the well-being of their fellow countrymen.

Chapter One

GOING TO SEA

MY training, a period of six years, in electrical and mechanical engineering in Staffordshire, was enjoyable and an instructive time of my life. I was lucky in being able to start my working life learning engineering, something I always wanted to do.

After an errand boy's job at a printers, it was arranged that I would serve an apprenticeship with a small firm, T M Birkett & Sons, Brassfounders and Engineers, Hanley, Staffordshire, who had a workforce of between 300 and 350 people. The chief engineer was responsible for my training and I started as the 'boy' in the small power station which supplied all the energy for the firm during working hours. Electricity from 'The Corporation' because it was expensive, was only used for lighting, for office cleaning, etc.

132 bhp horizontal and 84 bhp vertical oil engines at T M Birkett & Sons Ltd

My first job was to daily clean the red quarry floor, in the engine room, polish the brass and steel work around the one diesel engine, belt driving a direct current (DC) dynamo. Oiling the engine, making tea, running errands around the works to make me aware of the dangers in the foundry, machine shops, pattern shop, laboratory, stores, etc. During my apprenticeship I attended evening classes studying in the Senior Course in Electrical Engineering.

As I progressed in my training I was able to take over more responsible duties and during the latter two years, was the charge engineer responsible for the operation of the small power house which now had three diesel generators. All maintenance work had to be done at weekends after the factory shut down at midday on Saturday, or holiday periods. This meant that on many Saturdays and Sundays I had to work (maintenance experience) so my working week very often exceeded 66 hours. On occasions when a breakdown occurred it entailed 24-hour working. Overtime was paid at time and a quarter (3½d an hour), so with evening classes three times a week (with homework), during the winter months my pleasure activities were minimal. The highlight of the winter months was a 1/6d seat in the balcony at a local cinema on a Saturday night during summer time, on the odd Sunday, with a rambling club, exploring the Derbyshire Dales.

Potential flyer? No, future mariner

Rambling Club

When I became of age (21), and completed my apprenticeship, it followed that I would become eligible to receive a 'journeyman's' wage (£2-10s for a 48-hour week), but the weeks passed with only promises. Naturally, I was upset because for the past two years I had been helping to maintain and repair DC motors and switchgear within the works as well as design and build small generator distribution switchboards for outside contracts. I decided to look for another job.

Two representatives who regularly visited the firm, one from English Electric, Rugby, and the other from British Petroleum, suggested I apply to their firms and they would make their recommendations. The EEC representative thought the high tension switchgear design department would be suitable with my training and would speak to the manager on my behalf. Mr MacLean of BP who was an ex-chief engineer from the Blue Star Line, thought I would be ideally suited for the Mercantile Marine. I knew of a number of chief engineers of firms in the potteries, mining, steel works and silk mills who were all ex-marine engineers and after listening to some of Mr MacLean's world travel stories, his offer was given the first priority.

I have no doubt that his telephone conversation with Mr J Douglas, BSL, chief engineering superintendent carried weight, because within a few weeks I was invited, the week the letter arrived, to join the *Tacoma Star* at Hull. Such short notice made it impracticable for me to terminate my employment with T M Birkett & Sons. My letter of apology was answered with an instruction to report to BSL, St Mary Axe, in a fortnight's time.

A flurry of activity followed preparing 'Young Swain' for sea, with much sadness from my mother, but with the excitement of adventure on my part, I was leaving Burslem for foreign parts!

Burslem Old Town Hall

Having travelled a considerable amount with my parents in England, did not dim the aura I experienced travelling by train, tube and bus to present myself, complete with small suitcase with my raincoat strapped to it, to the BSL's St Mary Axe office. The commissionaire in his splendid uniform with medal ribbons and military greeting made me feel I should have saluted him! I don't think I had seen such pomp and circumstance at any office in Stoke-on-Trent! However, it was soon established I should report to the Chief Engineer of the *Stuart Star* berthed in the Royal Victoria Docks. Thank goodness I had had some previous experience of travel in London because trying to ask the average Londoner directions was hopeless, any district off their 'beaten track' was sometimes never heard of! A cultural shock to me, having been 'brought up' in an area of small towns, where a high percentage of people were in walking or cycling distance of their work place.

After a bewildering tube and bus journey, many enquiries and negotiating the bustle of dockland traffic, I found the *Stuart Star*, in the Victoria Dock, towering above me, discharging frozen meat. She was a lot bigger than the Isle of Man Steam Packets on which I had made a few trips on holidays as a teenager!

Mr Francis (chief engineer) welcomed me aboard, and after a brief period questioning me about my experience, showed me to my cabin. I was a little taken aback when he informed me the *Stuart* was a steam driven turbine ship, whereas I had been expecting, from my experience, to be appointed to a 'motor' ship. I had often heard the expression of one being on a learning curve, but my first week onboard the *Stuart* made me realise that mine was going to be a straight vertical line and would only begin to curve downwards in the months to follow!

The monthly pay of £13, with food and accommodation, had been a substantial improvement to my financial status, but when I found that in addition to my normal work-day hours, I had to keep a watch onboard 'duty engineer', it reduced my gain. Depending upon the number of assistant engineers available, a 24-hour watch aboard including Saturday afternoon and Sundays, had to be worked every third or fourth day, sometimes a senior engineer would take a turn. However, I had so much to learn that the extra duty periods were spent down in the engine room making diagrams of the many pipework systems, and learning the operations of all the auxiliary machinery.

My first inspection down below took me 'aback', I had never seen so much machinery and pipework packed into such a confined space, and that was only the engine room! In the stokehold I was impressed with the size of the 20-foot diameter Scotch boilers, two single and two double ended, towering above me into the darkness, and knowing this would be my domain at sea. One boiler always in port slightly vibrating supplying steam to the winches and auxiliary machinery and indicating the power which would be released at sea, when all would be gently throbbing.

The duty engineer was responsible in port for all the working machinery, boiler, auxiliary pumps, bilge, sanitary, fresh and salt water services, DC dynamo, winches and fire protection/fighting systems, so I had a lot to learn. Shipboard terminology had to be understood, and to be able to find one's way around the ship's many decks and spaces: orlop, shelter, tween and lower hold, masthouse, poop and so on were foreign parts to me. Directions to find them weren't much help until I had learnt to 'hold my port glass always in my left hand', and the for'd and aft were OK while one could see the blunt or sharp ends of the vessel. Down below where datum marks were not visible, it was very confusing.

The discharge of bananas, oranges and chilled beef had taken place before I joined the ship and the final consignment of frozen meat left the ship at the weekend. We then moved ship to a berth in the Royal Albert Dock where general cargo was loaded for Rio de Janeiro, Santos, Montevideo and Buenos Aires. In a few days time I would be on my maiden voyage, but during the past two weeks I had been trying to adapt to my totally strange environment. Fortunately one of the five new assistant engineers took me under his wing and helped me immensely (Mr Doonan). He was an ex-shipyard apprentice and had been to sea for a few months previously.

Visits by a marine tailor (Oliver's) had taken my measurements and quickly supplied a patrol, two tropical uniforms, three white boilersuits, uniform cap, white shoes, socks, and many other items which I needed. The tailor's account was settled by a credit note of payment vouched for by the BSL. I was now in debt to over one month's salary – something much against the grain, and the first time in my life for such a large amount, which

I knew would have met with my father's strong disapproval. However, there was no alternative, my new independence would not allow me to ask for a family loan.

Working on unfamiliar machinery was demanding, but I found the other new assistant engineers (first trippers), with the exception of Mr Doonan, were similarly placed, as they had come from non-marine backgrounds. They were from Scotland, Tyneside, Yorkshire and the Shetlands, so one had to listen carefully, in the noisy background of the engine room, to understand what was being said, even my North Staffordshire accent had to be toned down!

What with medical checks and signing on (for a voyage not exceeding two years!) at the shipping office and obtaining a Continuous Certificate of Discharge book, another outgoing expense of 2/6d, there was never a dull moment. We were informed sailing day would be Saturday 24 April 1937 and given arrival/departure dates with postal addresses for the South American ports Rio de Janeiro, Santos, Montevideo and Buenos Aires. I thought that the dates given were a rough guide because I considered it was optimistic to be able to sail thousands of nautical miles through spring, tropical and into autumn weather in the southern hemisphere and return punctually, when much shorter train journeys were difficult to maintain on time. When I voiced my thoughts to Mr Roberts, the second engineer officer whose assistant I would be on his 4–8 watch said 'Mr Swain, if the ship is not on schedule at all the ports of call, the skipper and chief engineer will be in trouble and if we're not on the right tide in the Thames on Wednesday (7 weeks hence), "heads will roll"'. He explained that most of the bananas and oranges would then be distributed to all parts of the country for the weekend markets. More importantly, the chilled beef must be on night express trains to be on sale in northern England, Scotland and Wales for the following Thursday morning.

During the last day of loading two wooden huts were built on the after deck to house polo ponies which were to be delivered to the Argentine. The stalls were narrow and insides padded so the horses could lean against them but could not lie down. I thought with the three weeks' voyage, standing would have been tiring but apparently no problem for the horses. Pedigree bulls were exported, to maintain the blood strain, in a similar manner, but the much heavier animals were supported with bands attached to the roofs passing under their bellies to take some of the weight off their legs.

Watch-keeping duties had been started, raising steam on two additional boilers (outward bound one single-ended was not required, but would be necessary for the demands of the refrigerating plant homewards). Being called at one bell (1/4 hour before every watch) was no problem for me, but some individuals were always difficult to get down below on time.

The first two watches and many more to follow were stressful carrying out my stokehold duties with frequent checks by Mr Roberts, but long before we reached the Bay of Biscay, the movement of the ship was beginning to make me feel a little queasy. I'm sure the tension and anxieties of having to master my new responsible duties, in the hot oil smelling atmosphere, contributed to my being completely sea sick on my third watch. I was given no respite by Mr Roberts, who instructed me: 'Don't forget, one hand for yourself and one for the company!', when I had to clamber up the fiddley, with a wheel key, to shut off the deck steam service.

Mounted on the stallion

Polo ponies

When he found me being sick in a stokehold bilge, he was most annoyed, and instructed me to always be sick in a wet bilge. This meant staggering through the engine room and about 30 yards down the propeller tunnels to the stern end, where the ship's movement was the greatest and always had a leakage of sea water through the propeller shaft gland. Needless to say, I made many trips during the watch, with annoyance from the second who had to see if I had carried out my duties correctly. For two days I had very little to eat and was advised to try and eat so that I had something to be sick with! In the event of my feeling a tube in my mouth, to hang onto it because it was my stern coming through!

When I eventually turned up in the engineers' dining room for a little food I was advised by the senior engineers to eat all sorts of nutritious dishes starting with nice fat bacon, etc, which quickly terminated my presence. But true to their forecast, within hours I was eating everything before me. Maintaining a watch, even when desperately sick, was an important lesson, to stop being sorry for oneself and continuing on the job accelerates recovery.

Sailing southwards we were soon in warmer weather with welcoming sunshine and I was beginning to enjoy my free time between watchkeeping duties. However, Mr Roberts, the second engineer, informed me, on a morning watch, that he had allocated to me No 4 hold's six beautiful, black, greasy and rusty steam winches to be maintained and repaired by me during the voyage. He expected that two hours each morning for five days outward and a similar stint homeward would enable me to keep them in good order and added that any breakdown in port would be my responsibility. He continued saying how lucky I was to have winches on the after deck because Nos 1, 2 and 3 holds' winches were subjected to longer submerged periods of sea water during rough weather especially a loaded ship, which was not helpful to their mechanical wellbeing. My financial gain going to sea had been further eroded.

It was during my first 'field days' as they were affectionately called, that I learnt a few first class engineering skills were needed. One was to split, what remained of hexagon nuts with a hammer and chisel when cylinder covers had to be removed, spanners were useless. Later on I was to find, on several occasions, I had to carry out breakdown repairs in port, vividly recalling one time in Buenos Aires. On returning to the ship in the early hours, after a wonderful night out, the duty engineer greeted me with the pleasant news that one of my winches needed first aid and would be required shortly when loading recommenced. So it was off with the glad rags and on with a boilersuit, thankfully my stalwart companions with whom I had shared the joys of the previous hours joined me similarly rigged and the job was quickly finished. Work hard, play hard, together, was a custom I was to learn from my seafaring days.

To see winches working in the hands of skilled stevedores always fascinated me and I was amazed how they continued to function continuously with only infrequent breakdown under such demanding work loads. The way loaded slings or trays were transferred from the vertical to the horizontal, traverse across the deck to be either lowered down onto quay or into hatch, was a delight to watch. Perfect co-ordination was necessary between both winch operators to ensure that take-up and pay-off were equal, otherwise instant overload to wires, shackles or even derricks could occur with disastrous results. Also to see downward plummeting loads brought to a gentle touch-down by throwing the winch into reverse with only a touch of the brake; it illustrated the ability of steam to cushion and give instant power in the opposite direction. An asset which I was to appreciate later in my career when on rare occasions a FULL ASTERN from ahead was telegraphed from bridge to the engine room. Something main steam reciprocating engines could provide with no problem; no need to shut off steam but just throw over the reversing links with an immediate change in rotation, albeit with a resentful groan and hiss from the engine. Something during my time the diesels or turbines could not emulate.

Swimming bath with steam winches behind

Sailing through the tropics in the engine room was another 'mind barrier' to overcome and an unpleasant experience. The temperature and humidity progressively increased along with my insatiable thirst. Again I thought I would never survive, but sound advice not to drink too much, especially cold water, was hard to follow. When I saw senior officers in the dining room putting salt in their water glasses, I couldn't believe my eyes, but it was explained to me that it was necessary to replace the lost salt from the body due to excessive perspiration (confirmed years later, during the Second World War, when salt tablets were issued to combat heat exhaustion). Nevertheless, when the temperature began to fall, life became a little more comfortable, but on deck to limit one's exposure to the sun which was made deceptive by the cooling breeze caused by the ship's speed (15 knots). We did have the luxury of a swimming bath which consisted of a canvas bag, about three yards square, supported in a sturdy wooden frame. It had to be used with care as there was only a small outside ladder with a single post with which to enter and when the ship was rolling the sea water depth could vary from three feet to one being floated over the top.

When I was told that the following morning we would be arriving at the first foreign port Rio de Janeiro, I was excited and when I came off watch the evening before, I had my first experience of seeing a dull glow in the black star-lit sky and the first smell of tropical vegetation on an off-shore breeze, a never to be forgotten moment!

The vista of Rio harbour with the Sugar Loaf and Corcovado overlooking the beautiful bays was exciting coupled with the new smells, sounds and seeing the exotic vegetation of my first foreign port. Our stay was short and

The Corcovado

Figure of Christ

I only had a few hours ashore accompanied by two assistant engineers, mainly to have a quick look round and to post our first letters home. We soon found finding one's way difficult because only Portuguese was spoken, and my first embarrassing mistake was going into the wrong lavatory in the tourist building!

After some difficulty we found the post office, letters handed in with a Milreis note (value £2) and I was given a handful of coins with stamps for my two airmail letters. I thought it seemed a small amount. Fortunately shortly after leaving the post office we met Mr Lee the 'third' a New Zealander and on showing him my change, he told me I had got the equivalent of 10d in my hand! So he accompanied us back to the post office and after some angry gesticulation with the Maori greeting thrown in, the clerk handed over the rest of my change (notes). Apparently, it was common practice when the clerks could see they were dealing with a 'green' foreigner and we were also warned to make sure the stamps were properly stuck on because it was common practice to remove them for re-sale!

The wonderful sights and beauty of Rio made up for the small language problems and our resort to miming resulted in funny episodes. For example, in our first café, requiring milk for our coffee, we mimed milking a cow which was eventually brought by the waiter who had never seen such sacrilege, spoiling the strong black Brazilian coffee.

Santos the old yellow fever port was another experience sailing up river and the difficult manoeuvre turning the ship with the bow on the quay against a fast-flowing river. I managed to walk round the park in the small town welcoming the shade of the palms which I had never seen before and the indescribable smells of the tropical vegetation. We loaded bananas on deck for the short sea passage to the River Plate, where after a few hours at Montevideo, made the long passage to Buenos Aires. This required two-hour stand-by watches in addition to the normal four, sailing up the buoyed channel in the wide yellow river. I understood that it was kept navigable, with minimal dredging, by the constant passage of 'beef' ships like the *Stuart.*

So we arrived at our terminal port Buenos Aires in the South Dock, where we would be for ten days after the final discharge of our general cargo and bananas from Santos. The refrigeration department would now be at its busiest cooling down spaces to accept the frozen and chilled beef. The huge Anglo-Frigerifico dominated the quay and the smell reminded me of the one from a Bovril bottle; one could also hear the continuous bellowing of cattle in the many stockyards behind the 'meat works'. Sea-going watches were broken and day-work started and during the days to follow, much maintenance carried out on the turbines and boilers by the ship's engineers with some of the larger jobs done by the Central, the BSL's repair workshops. I was to meet and work alongside Spanish-speaking engineers and fitters who were usually surrounded with a strong smell of garlic. Some had a smattering of English, but one had to quickly learn the Spanish engineering terms.

I vaguely remember my first trip into town with companions which was some miles from the South Dock. After passing through the dock gates guarded by police, who invariably requested gifts of cigarettes - we walked along a dirt road passing small shacks selling fruit, curios, etc. I was warned that it was always wise to be accompanied when returning to the ship late at night/early morning because 'The Boca' had a reputation for violent incidents.

Unloading bananas - BA

Stuart *loading alongside the* Anglo

We had to cross the river using the 'transporter' the first time I had seen this type of bridge. It consisted of a section of roadway suspended from a high steel gantry which bridged the river. The gondola containing a couple of small lorries and pedestrians would then traverse across the water on its wheeled bogey high above. I believe it was a replica of a similar transporter across the Tees in England.

Before going ashore I was warned, that in the event of being near a car accident, and there were many, not to let my curiosity retain my presence, but to beat a hasty retreat from the scene. It was the policy of the police to arrest the drivers concerned and all the potential witnesses for questioning which could mean losing one's liberty for many hours. I was also told, not many years before the advent of the motor car, fines for minor misdemeanours meant carrying out menial chores like cleaning out the many stables and sweeping the streets. Apparently the skipper and chief engineer of a BSL vessel who had imbibed to excess, were seen by members of their crew sweeping one of the main avenues in BA! Embarrassment was, no doubt, a good deterrent and perhaps could have the same effect today. I was also advised that some establishments with coloured lights outside were not all dentists' surgeries!

Our first port of call, after crossing the river was *Whites* for a beer and to get small change for the 'colectivos' to take us to town. The 'cerveza' was a lager containing large quantities of froth which the barman had to constantly remove with a wooden spatula and usually had a few glasses filling at the same time, in order to obtain a full glass of lager. Toasted peanuts, well salted in their shells, were always served in small dishes with the drinks. It was a feature in all the bars where floors had to be constantly swept to remove the carpet of discarded shells, which occurred during busy periods. In *Whites* there was a small glass case on the wall containing a sprig of hops. On enquiry I was told it was on display and dipped in the brew now and again to satisfy the constant complaints from the British clientele that there was no taste of hops in the frothy lager!

The first destination in town was usually the main post office having survived a fast bumpy ride in an overcrowded colectivo. There were many and I think mostly privately owned by the drivers who, competing for customers, raced one another with their 30-35 passengers (seats for 20), no shock-absorbers working, over the poor suburban streets. One of the main avenues leading to the post office was lined with curio shops, bars, etc, which were set back, providing a covered pavement and was always called 'under the arches'. It was an international meeting place and provided for all sorts of tastes, something like Soho in London.

As a young man coming from a sheltered life in a small provincial town I was shocked by some of the goings on, my educational curve was given a sharp vertical peak! There were so many experiences in sound, smells, sights and to me strange customs that must be left for another story. At the cinema mostly American films were shown and contrarily to British custom, no smoking was allowed, but at the intervals a quick exit was made to the foyer where one could smoke. Large ashtrays and sand boxes were provided so when the bell rang announcing the programme was about to start, cigarettes could be safely disposed. I believe the reason for this practice was the high insurance premiums incurred if smoking were permitted in the auditorium.

On all the level main and secondary streets car parking was allowed, but drivers had to leave hand brakes inoperative. This allowed closer parking, the practice being to shunt the adjacent cars front and rear using the bumpers until an exist could be made. Most of the cars were American, but when the odd British car, the bumpers of which were below the level of the huge chromium plated limos, suffered some mangling during the shunting process!

Exploring the wonderful city, at the time claimed to be the largest in the southern hemisphere, was my main interest and I soon learned that the evening entertainment started around 10.00 pm. We soon made the practice of taking a couple of hours sleep after our evening meal before going shore-side. The local workforce used to take at least a two-hour siesta midday and the custom for families with very young children dining out could be seen in the restaurants late at night.

At Montevideo the ship I was later to sail in – Avelona Star

A well-known restaurant whose reputation for its 'beefy caballero' was often visited for dinner, but the size and thickness of the succulent beef (2-3 inches thick), was too much for me even when a small portion was ordered. It was remarkable to see the large portions of meat eaten by the average Argentinian because I suppose of its cheapness. In the foyer of the restaurant stood a life-size replica of a short-horned Angus bull which was often mounted by well-satisfied and happy customers. Rumour had it that a well-known BSL 'super' sometimes gave a very realistic demonstration of a Gaucho with bolas capturing a steer!

Eventually the *Stuart* left BA loaded with frozen and chilled beef. In the engine room all sea water intakes opened on to high injection to ensure a continuous flow of cooling water, because frequently the ship would ground during the passage down river when passing other vessels in the narrow channel, sometimes maintaining a slight list for minutes until she cleared the sandy bottom. More frozen meat was taken on at Montevideo as the ship's draught could be increased because a deep-water passage was now available. The port of Santos contributed bananas and oranges to our homeward bound cargo.

After leaving Santos, on the way to Rio, we spent a day at anchor in the shelter of the Isle de Sao Sebastiao. It was a lovely day and a beautiful setting, surrounded by hills covered with lush vegetation of many hues of green. Barges, ferried out with small tugs were loaded with crates of oranges and stalks of bananas, which I understood came from plantations owned by the Vestey family. Our deck hands acted as stevedores, manning the steam winches and local labour stowing the oranges in the holds. Due to the chief officer's men being unfamiliar with working the winches, the transfer of the loaded sling trays (24-30 boxes) at first was anything but smooth! Many cases of fruit were cascaded onto the deck, oranges rolling everywhere from the burst boxes. Trying to replace and repair the damaged cargo was out of the question as the loading had to progress as quickly as possible, so oranges were sampled by all hands and after peeling the first few, orange juice became the drink of the day. Water decanters in the accommodation were kept filled with the delicious juice, but I remember our Irish doctor commenting at the time that 'we young men should curtail our intake of the citrus juice because it could seriously affect our concupiscence!'

We departed the 'Orange Juice Anchorage' and the next day arrived at Rio de Janeiro. Again the main cargo was bananas and oranges. Shore visits were limited because at most intermediate ports, only hours alongside, sea-going watches were maintained. The 4-8 watch, however, did allow a reasonable period of free time after breakfast to explore. I was able to visit the Corcovado which from the ship looked like a cross on the hill and dominated the backdrop surrounding the beautiful harbour. On arrival by road and rack and pinion railway, one could see the cross was a huge stone figure of Christ with out-stretched arms which dominated the panorama of hills and sea inlets, which provided many safe, deep-water anchorages. The many wonderful views from the Corcovado will always remain in my memory.

IN THE SHELTER OF THE ISLE DE SAO SEBASTIAO

Loading a sling of oranges with a banana conveyor behind

Mr Doonan, in the distance the despatch jetty

The rest of the homeward-bound voyage was still a stressful period for me, still learning amid the 'spit and polish' activities preparing the engine and boiler rooms to arrive in London clean and sparkling in every direction: from the illuminated white painted tank-tops under the boilers, to show immediately any leakage of fuel oil from a malfunctioning burner, to the polished hand-wheels, floorplates, brass pressure gauges and gleaming blue planished steel casings of the turbines. Paintwork everywhere had been 'sujied' or re-painted in all areas including awkward places behind machinery. Cleanliness, a major contribution towards safety especially against fire, gave one a sense of pride and wellbeing, in the dangerous confined spaces.

After passing Cape Finistere an atmosphere of pleasure pervaded the ship traditionally called the 'Channels'. On reaching Dungeness to pick up our channel pilot, in the engine room stand-by watches commenced and would continue until we docked. This entailed an additional two hours to the normal four, but was essential to accommodate speed changes in the busy shipping lanes. In the event of an emergency to be prepared to stop and give full astern power on receiving a double ring full astern on the telegraph. At Gravesend the channel pilot left and the docking pilot took over, at the same time gangs of riggers came on board whom, during the river passage prepared the ship for unloading. Tarpaulins, hatchboards were removed, derricks unshipped and trimmed so that the discharge of bananas and chilled beef could commence immediately the ship was alongside her berth in the Royal Victoria Dock. A real sense of urgency prevailed getting our valuable cargo speeding on its way to all parts of Britain.

So my first voyage was over after seven weeks of excitement, trauma and so many new experiences packed in such a short time. Overall, my enthusiasm to continue this new life was much diminished and was also shared by the other four assistant engineers who all resigned their service with the BSL. In my case I decided to make another voyage, the main factors being the determination to have another go and as I had spent half my salary to date, on uniform, etc, at least further outlay would be minimal, so another two months' voyage would give me some return on my investment.

The next trip proved to be so different, even with only two months' sea service, it gave me a sense of seniority over the four new assistant engineers all of whom were 'first trippers'. More importantly, I seemed to meet with some approval from Mr Roberts on whose watch I remained. Another small benefit was also made when 'crossing the line' on the next voyage. There was no elaborate ceremony like those performed on passenger ships when crossing the equator. On the *Stuart*, first trippers were asked in the mess whether they had felt the bump during the night as the ship crossed the equator? The new boys were expected to stand a round of drinks for the old hands. So I was on the receiving end and would be for future trips. It was interesting to see the new fourth engineer officer, Mr Middleditch, also stand a round even though he had been at sea a few years and carried a 'second's ticket' but had never crossed the equator. All his previous voyages had been from the UK to Japan and the nearest to the equator were the times he had passed through the Singapore Straits!

On the outward passage, somewhere in the 'Doldrums' the skipper altered the *Stuart*'s course in order to pass on the lee-side of a sailing ship - a rare sight. She was underway, the wisp of a breeze just filling her sails and made a magnificent sight. I was able to take three pictures as we steamed past her, she was the *Schuleshiff Deutchland* identifying her as one of Germany's training ships for naval officers. I believe some 150 cadets manned her with their officers. The usual courtesy was exchanged, Ensigns dipped, etc. Little did we think at the time that most, if not all of the young cadets would be officers in the Germany Navy and in just two years' time would be our enemies. A few could have been potential U-boat captains, despatching their 'tin fish' aiming to hit the engine rooms of our ships without warning and the loss of many lives during the 'War at Sea'.

Schuleshiff Deutchland *German Naval training ship*

Rio was further explored on subsequent voyages and travelling to the top of the Sugar Loaf a new experience. It was the first time I had been in a cable car, so the trip to the summit via the intermediate station on top of another adjacent rock exciting; also swinging in the air at a great height was unique, and the panoramic views wonderful.

On my third voyage to BA we found a profound change had taken place in the South American city's way of life. To we foreigners the glamour and perhaps over-free society had dramatically changed to a sombre austere form when President Peron came to power.

ASCENDING THE SUGAR LOAF

Sugar Loaf from the intermediate station

The intermediate station

Near the top

Chapter Two

THE LAST VOYAGE OF THE *STUART STAR*

I WAS now beginning to settle down to my new life and used my free time at sea to study for a second class Board of Trade Certificate of Competency, I had much to learn. In November 1937, we learned that our next voyage was to Australia via South Africa steaming outward bound on coal and returning on oil. Most large steam ships had been using oil firing for some years, so the conversion of the *Stuart*'s boilers to coal firing was perhaps unique. At that time, bunkering oil was imported into Australia and its high cost made it economically justifiable to change to coal firing and increase the stokehold crew for the longer voyage.

The normal stokehold staff on oil were two firemen on each watch (six), on coal six firemen, two trimmers and a 'peggy', making a total of 27 men. So, accommodation, food and wages for the four months' voyage had to be provided for the extra 21 men. I was told that the *Stuart* had made similar voyages before, and one of the problems for the Second Engineer and the Mate was finding sufficient work to keep the 21 surplus men gainfully employed homeward bound.

No 2 and 3 holds were used as coal bunkers filled in the UK, oil bunkers and double-bottoms filled at Cape Verde Isles on the outward passage. Around the Australian coast as the coal was used the boilers were progressively converted to oil firing, an arduous task for the ship's engineers, in addition to their normal duties.

We left Liverpool on 20 November 1937 and the passage out to South Africa was uneventful, but my learning curve was given a vertical 'blip'. None of we assistants, or, indeed some of the senior officers, had had coal-firing experience and coal firemen were few and far between - No wonder when a comparison is made between coal and oil firing for the same pay!

The two oil firemen on each watch had to clean 24 oil burners, after which no further physical work was necessary. Coal firing was a different 'kettle of fish', it was a continuous hard slog in hot, dirty conditions for the same pay. I quickly found that the only way to lead the men and carry the steam 'on the blood' under these conditions, was to be able to fire a boiler as good as they; learning how to use the slice, jumbo-rake and shovel and to understand stokehold terminology eg 'B– ol' man on the back-end' and 'on the rattle', etc. Also, as their vocabularies were limited and supplemented by many four-letter words, it was necessary to be able to use the latter so that a degree of understanding was established between oneself and the men.

When on oil the *Stuart*'s average speed was 14–15 knots, but on coal it was difficult to maintain 13 knots. The necessity to clean at least six fires each watch meant, for the first and last hour of each watch, the steaming

The Stuart Star

capability was much reduced. Consequently we were two days behind schedule on reaching Cape Town.

On Friday 17 December 1937 when the ship was nearing East London it became foggy during the morning. When I came off watch, after 8.00am, I could see in the distance the tops of hills above the fog bank. As was my practice, if no 'field day' duties were required, after breakfast I would take a short nap on my settee. A sudden jolt and the engine room emergency bells in the adjacent alleyway must have awakened me. Donning a boilersuit over my underpants and 'chain-breaker' vest, I slid down the flights of engine room ladders joining the watch-keeping engineers.

The vessel had already developed a starboard list and the heavy swell was causing the ship to shudder violently because (as was later found), she was firmly held on the rocks at the for'd end. The situation was frightening, especially for the younger engineers like myself. We were fortunate having Mr Brandie, the second engineer, who encouraged and led us with a nonchalant approach to the serious and difficult conditions which worsened during the next five hours. (Sadly I believe he was lost with 72 others when the *Avila Star* was sunk by U-201 in July 1942.) In order to maintain steam, the first priority was to get as much coal as we could from No 3 hold through the watertight door into the stokehold. This procedure was speeded up because water started pouring into the hold shortly after grounding. When the inflow of water mixed with fuel oil increased rapidly, the watertight door was closed. In the meantime we had been told that tugs from East London were coming out to our assistance and that we should be prepared to give full astern power when telegraphed.

Two attempts to pull the *Stuart* off the rocks were made by the tugs with our main turbines giving maximum astern power. The first attempt was aborted when the tugs' hawser parted, and the second attempt was maintained for some time, I think for 20 minutes but was finally abandoned.

During this time conditions in the stokehold and engine room deteriorated, the constant shuddering movement each time waves hit the starboard side made it difficult to maintain one's foothold on the sloping floor plates, (varying from 30° to 40°) as the level of oily water rose in engine room and stokehold.

HOOD POINT

Twenty minutes after grounding

Forty minutes later

Tugs standing by

Spectators watching

Unfortunately the two steam driven DC generators in the engine room were on the starboard side, one at floor plate level and the other about three feet higher on a platform. Soon the water level rose above the floor plates making it necessary to shut down the lower generator. Later the second machine had to be switched off. From then on we had no electric lighting, but daylight through the engine room skylight made it possible to move around the centre platform but hand torches were needed in the wings. In the stokehold they were essential to enable us to carry out our duties but it was still difficult climbing up in the fiddleys to see that each boiler gauge glass had water in it.

Pumping the stokehold bilges had started shortly after the grounding but despite using all the pumping services the water level soon approached the lower fireboxes on the starboard boiler. A dangerous situation because any in-rush of water into the fireboxes (still filled with burning coal) could cause a blow-back, probably blowing off the cast iron doors! It was thought that coal/ash was now blocking the bilge suctions so I was instructed to remove the bilge valve covers which were already under water and positioned just opposite the fireboxes where the water level was only inches below!

Mr McMahon, another assistant engineer, was with me. He was on the 12-4 and as there was a personality clash between us, we were not on good terms. When I took over from him on watch, we had a different interpretation on the amount of fuel left in the settling tanks. There was keen competition between watches because the fuel consumption showed how efficient the stokehold engineer had been with his combustion management. He was a dour Scot and big with it! My attempts to remove the bilge valve covers under a foot of water coated with bunker oil was not easy by torch light and the knowledge that a minor explosion could occur at any moment from the fireboxes behind me didn't help! Mr McMahon pulled me away from the dangerous position and carried on with me handing the tools to him from a safe distance until the covers were removed. I held him in high regard from then on. During times of danger often undiscovered weakness or strength of character is revealed. It was a lesson I have never forgotten.

The situation continued to worsen in stokehold and engine room, the water level increasing despite bilge, general service and ballast transfer pumps working full power on the bilge lines. As the list to starboard increased the starb'd boiler was isolated and steam pressure released by jacking (lifting) the safety valves. It was obvious the water level in No 3 hold had increased rapidly because the resultant pressure was causing the watertight door to leak badly and at various points above from holes in the bulkhead. Jets of water were cascading down onto the floor-plates making it difficult for us to avoid getting drenched. 'Chippy' was sent for who managed to reduce some of the leakage by plugging and wedging the watertight door. The ship continued to judder violently, lack of daylight, the smell of fuel oil, the noise of escaping steam and the knowledge that the ship could keel over any moment, provided a stressful condition for all hands.

Sea water had now reached the centre-line tunnel between stokehold and engine room. It must have been two hours after the grounding when the two centre-line, single ended boilers were isolated, de pressurised, leaving only the port boiler in operation. It was supplying steam to all the pumps and in addition, the starb'd Gwynne (main condenser circulating pump), which had been put on bilge injection with the sea inlet closed. This pump was able to suck large volumes of water from the engine room and pump it directly overboard and at the time seemed to be holding the level of flooding. However, by about 2.00 pm it was obvious that despite the all-out effort to contain the in-rush of water, we were having to wade through two feet of water when passing through the tunnel between engine room and stokehold.

I think it was about 3.00 pm when we were told to abandon ship because the barometer had begun to fall and when the level of water was beginning to cover the starb'd turbine. It was then that we assistant engineers realised a dramatic clean-up was necessary before going topside; so we stripped off in the workshop discarding our oil soaked boiler suits, underwear, socks/shoes and washed each other down with paraffin using rags to get the majority of fuel oil off our bodies. It was also necessary to rinse our hair in a bucket of clean paraffin. I took a last look down as we climbed the ladders, naked, cringing from the uncomfortable feel of the hot oily rungs of the gratings, I could see the compound two-cylinder engine driving the main circulating pump still running under water! It was fascinating to see the cranks, connecting rods and eccentrics moving under water as if on normal service, presumably the port boiler was still supplying steam from its residual heat and remains of burning coal in the fireboxes. (One wonders if modern electrically driven auxiliaries would function totally immersed, provided power were still available.)

We were ordered to pack a minimum of clothing and personal belongings as quickly as possible and to stand-by to be taken off by the lifeboat from East London. It used the *Stuart Star*'s port side which provided a lee to the heavy inshore swell. As we walked along the deck to disembark the extent of the damage and penetration of the rocks into the ship's double bottom tanks were indicated by the bilge sounding pipes. They were pushed out above the deck level some three to four feet, Nos 1, 2 and 3 holds affected!

It was ironic to note that the *Stuart Star* had come to grief immediately opposite Hood Point Lighthouse which was only visible some twenty minutes after the grounding, when the fog had lifted. Unfortunately at that time the lighthouse had no fog warning apparatus because the incident of fog was very infrequent. I understand sound warning equipment was installed after the wreck.

The 15 passengers had been taken off during the morning and the majority of officers and men were ashore by late afternoon. Finding accommodation for everyone was difficult because it was the summer holiday season, hotels were full so we junior officers were kindly accommodated in the homes of people associated with seafaring activities. I was fortunate in being able to stay in, I think, the harbour master's or tug master's bungalow. An army camp hosted the ratings.

On visiting Hood Point the morning after the grounding it confirmed the wise decision to abandon the vessel because heavy seas were pounding the *Stuart*, they were breaking over the decks and one could see spray as high as the masts and funnel, getting a boat alongside would have been very difficult and dangerous.

THE DAY AFTER THE GROUNDING 18 DECEMBER 1937

Seas breaking over the foremast and bridge

Holiday visitors viewing the Stuart *from Hood Point*

Junior Officers with Cadets on left and right-hand sides

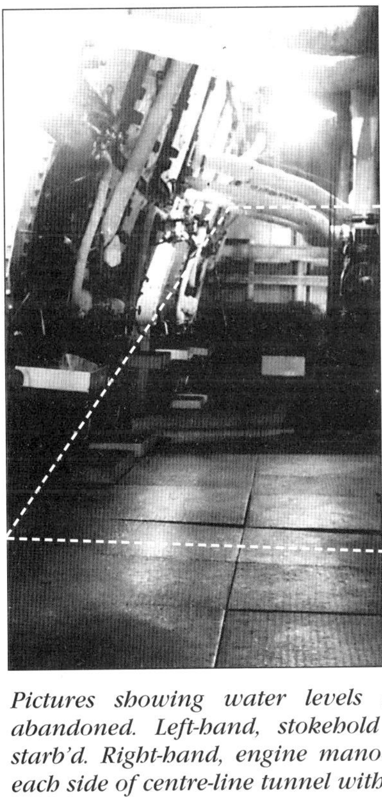

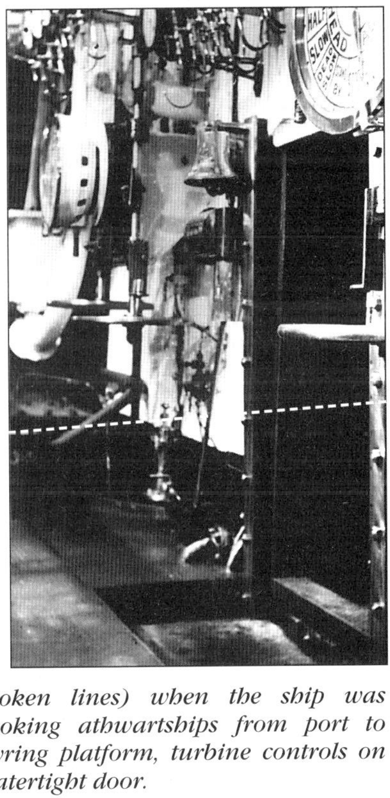

Pictures showing water levels (broken lines) when the ship was abandoned. Left-hand, stokehold looking athwartships from port to starb'd. Right-hand, engine manoeuvring platform, turbine controls on each side of centre-line tunnel with watertight door.

We spent a few days in East London and travelled back to the UK in the lap of luxury as first class passengers on the *mv Dunbar Castle*.

About a year later after the loss of the *Stuart Star*, I made another trip to Australia via South Africa, on the *mv Australia Star* which called at East London. I was able to get round to Hood Point and was amazed to see the damage to my old ship; the hull had been broken up into three separate sections, separation taking place just abaft the main engine room and again at the poop, the latter sections being some half a mile down the coast from the main part of the vessel.

ONE YEAR LATER

The bow and midships section

The aft well deck and poop

Chapter Three

Sailing Home in Style

AFTER the loss of the *Stuart Star* at East London on 17 December 1937, with the exception of the captain, chief engineer and specific officers and men required for the court of inquiry to be held at Cape Town, the remaining 83 crew members were shipped back to the UK as disabled British seamen.

It transpired that the Union Castle Line's intermediate vessel the *mv Dunbar Castle* was to be our passenger ship. She was a motor ship of 10,002 tons and when we joined her found she had already on board a large contingent of British Army personnel. They had completed a tour of duty on Mauritius, so the passenger list was predominantly made up of Army and Merchant Service people. We were met by first-class cabin stewards who conducted us to our cabins and informed us that dinner would be served in an hour and would we require assistance with dressing for dinner. Uniform

Later sunk by mine in the Thames Estuary during the War

would have been appropriate for us to wear but after making enquiries it was suggested that lounge suits would be acceptable and thereby maintain the ship's officers' identity with the passengers. Our cabin stewards departed informing us that should we require anything or service at any time they would be on call, and mine said he would call me at six in the morning when my bath would be ready.

Within the space of a few days we had been transposed from the austere cabin facilities of the *Stuart Star*, where a compactum provided a tank of cold water with a foldaway basin and a small can of hot water brought by a steward, to the luxurious well-appointed cabin with hand-basin and hot and

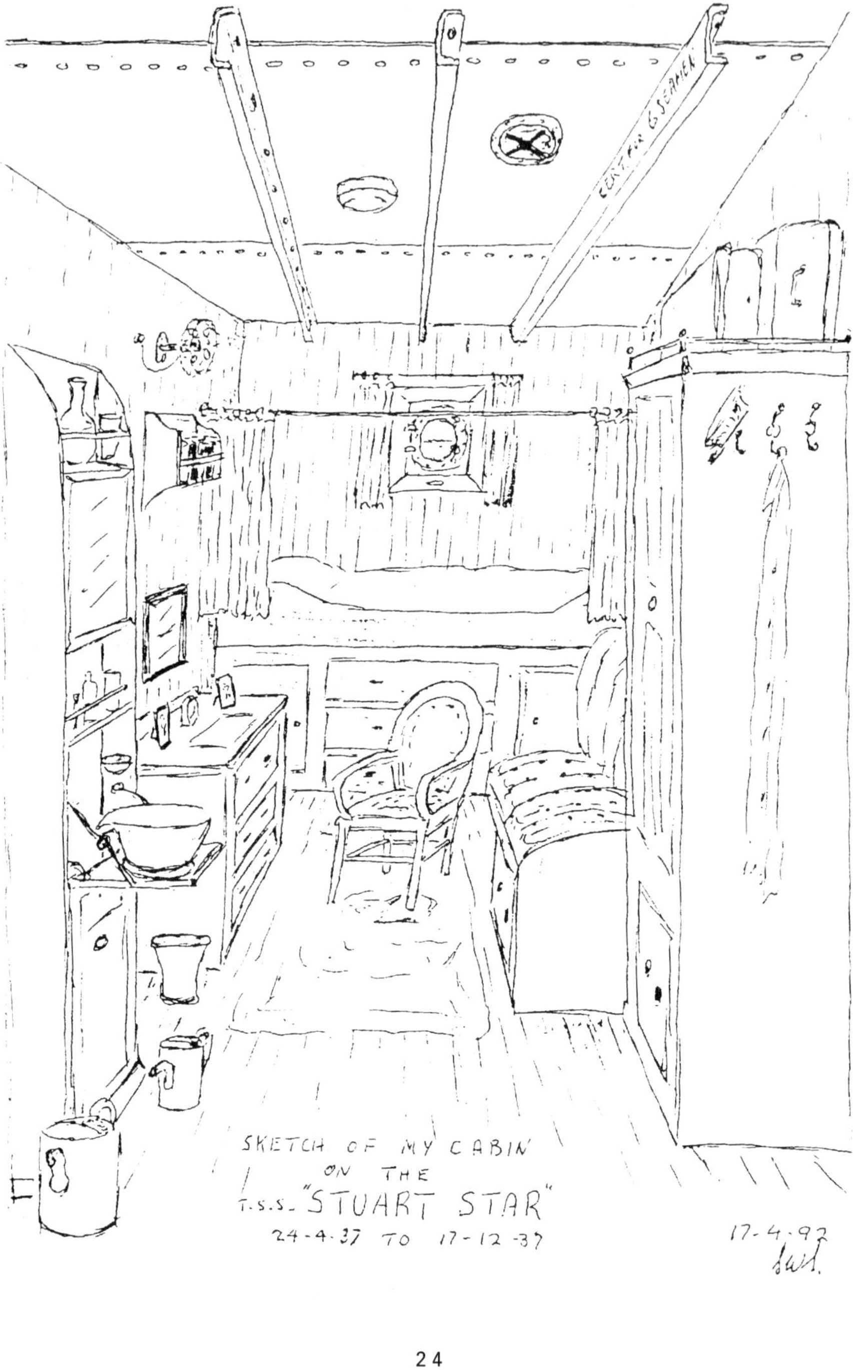
CENTRE FOR SEAMEN
SKETCH OF MY CABIN
ON THE
T.S.S. "STUART STAR"
24-4-37 TO 17-12-37
17-4-92

cold running water! In my case, the interim period of a few days staying in the harbour master's bungalow (a wooden building with corrugated iron roof) was also a unique experience being wakened one night by a roar of sound from heavy rain on the roof.

The first dinner aboard the *Dunbar Castle* was an occasion I shall never forget. One entered the dining saloon down a few steps onto a small dance floor surrounded by tables beautifully decorated with flowers, with an orchestra playing from a minstrels' gallery above the diners. We were ushered to a large table at one side of the dance floor by the head waiter (there were 12 of us), which seemed to be on view to all the diners (about 120). When I sat down at the table I was a little bewildered by the display of cutlery and number of wine glasses at each setting (a more common sight nowadays).

Wide coverage had been given by the local newspapers to the wreck of the *Stuart Star* accompanied with pictures of the ship on the rocks and crew members who had been accommodated in an Army barracks. Consequently our entry into the dining room was watched with keen interest, we being new passengers but also shipwrecked mariners making local history!

The splendour and atmosphere of the dining saloon with the colourful assembly, the ladies in their finery and the gentlemen in evening dress with a large sprinkling of military uniforms, made me feel a little self-conscious. It was obvious that my young companions were suffering in the same way; I had only been at sea eight months and some of them on their first voyage! Our waiter gave me a large beautifully decorated menu, on the cover was a picture of an exotic South African bird. I used it as a screen, but was thrown into greater confusion when I saw that the whole menu was written in French and the only English was printed on the opposite page giving the musical items to be played by the orchestra! Fortunately for me, Mr McLaughlin, another assistant engineer officer, was the first to be asked what he would like for his first course. 'Paddy', in desperation, pointed to the first item in English on the menu, to whom the waiter, in a very polite manner said: "I'm sorry Sir, but the orchestra is playing that now!"

At four bells the next morning I was called by my steward and found a hot salt water bath awaiting me; it was difficult to get a real lather with the salt water soap provided but I felt refreshed after my ablutions. We soon settled into the leisurely and sedate routine of our new-found ship-board life, but the bars and any activity which required cash were given a wide berth, so we concentrated on all sport activities. One of my colleagues, a 'keen blade', on the second evening after joining the ship, invited a young lady passenger for a drink at the bar. The next morning 'Jock' much chastened, described his short evening of anguish to us; apparently the young teenaged lady's favourite drink was double scotch and after a few drinks even at 'sea prices' our ship-mate ruefully slipped her cable. Our third engineer, Jock's senior watch-keeping officer, informed him that the young lady he had been entertaining was a Miss Peak, a member of the well-known Peak Freen Biscuit family, and suggested he would have to be a little more financially discerning on his choice of companions. Mr Findley proved to be a mine of information on the social scene because he was a man who enjoyed his pipe while sitting at the bar with a pint of beer close by. He was a fatherly figure in his twenty seventh year who advised us on how the parents (mostly Army) kept a watchful eye on their daughters and thereby steered us clear of potentially dangerous waters!

Not surprisingly, even though we entered full heartedly into all the sporting activities the life on-board soon became a little mundane so when a fancy dress ball was announced, we took an interest in its potential. This was stimulated because three of us with a male passenger had formed a friendly group with four lady passengers. I forget who suggested it, most probably one of the ladies, that they would like to borrow our tropical uniforms for the ball. Two of them, who were travelling together, found that with some tacks in strategic places, our uniforms would fit nicely (my boyish figure disappeared many years ago!).

Making new friends

Four hula-hula girls

Fancy dress costumes were available from the purser, of which most passengers took advantage but there was a hire charge. So we decided that the four of us would masquerade as Hawaiian maidens. Short lengths of new manila hawser were obtained from the *Dunbar*'s bosun and we spent many sessions teasing out the strands making hula-hula skirts to wear over our swimming trunks. It was surprising how long it took and the amount of rope needed for the skirts. Bra's from the ladies were loaned to us suitably extended with elastic tape to suit our 'fuller figures'. At a dress rehearsal, suitably made up, we tried to imitate hula-hula girls but no way could we either sway our hips or pass as girls! So we added bow ties to our bare necks, black socks with suspenders, black shoes, and notices attached to the skirts with the warnings 'NO BIRD NESTING' and 'NO SMOKING'.

The fancy dress ball was a huge success, the orchestra playing appropriate music to accompany the entrance of all the passengers in fancy dress, our two ladies to *Every girl loves a sailor* and the four of us to Hawaiian music whom the Naval officers picked up after our dance, and escorted us to our table.

Another event was a treasure hunt which provided an interesting time searching for about 50 listed items, some of which were obviously targeted to be difficult to find. One was a piece of coal and as the *Dunbar* was a motor ship and the galley oilfired, it proved to be impossible. However, I remembered that one of my firemen had shown me a small piece of coal he had always carried at sea as a lucky charm. After negotiating the segregating barriers I found him in the second class accommodation and after some difficulty, persuaded him to loan me his treasure. It proved to be the only time ever in the judicature's service on the ship that a piece of coal had been presented. Needless to say it was critically examined to make sure it was genuine.

Our passage of 12 days, at times became boring, it was an experience which taught me that even when travelling in the lap of luxury with every comfort, life soon became mundane. I made one or two visits to the engine room to break the monotony.

We arrived in the UK some days after Christmas and were given a few days leave. On my arrival home, I found that fortunately, my parents had received my first and only letter from South Africa after the loss of the *Stuart* on Christmas Eve. They said it was a wonderful Christmas present to know that I was really safe and well. Apparently on the day of the shipwreck (17 December 1937), it was reported on the 'wireless' on the BBC's 9.00pm news that all the passengers had been taken off the vessel, but only half of the crew. Naturally my parents thought that their 'boy' would be still on-board! Unlike today, telephones were sparsely placed, so my father went to the local police station. After many telephone calls, starting with the Blue Star Line's St. Mary Axe office, which was closed at that time of night, he finally established from Lloyds of Liverpool, that all crew members had been taken off and there was none injured. With great relief at two o'clock in the morning, my father was able to reassure my mother that her son was safe.

Chapter Four

CHASING THE *AUSTRALIA STAR*

AFTER the loss of the *Stuart Star* I made two voyages to Brazil and Argentina as an assistant engineer officer on the *Avelona Star*. Originally she had accommodation for 162 first-class passengers; in 1934 cabin and second funnel were removed and converted into cargo space.

Avelona Star

At the end of May 1938 I was looking forward to a few days leave, when on a Friday afternoon I was offered promotion to second refrigerating engineer on the *Australia Star*. Being ambitious but realising that my duties on the frig. would not count as sea-going time for my ticket, but knowing that experience on refrigeration was essential for BSL management, I accepted. 'When is she sailing?' I asked, 'Tomorrow afternoon' came the reply, so instead of going on leave to Staffordshire, I trundled my bags along the quay and was soon on my way to Australia!

Outward bound Mr (Canon) Brady, chief refrigerating engineer and I were responsible for the overhaul of the Brush four cylinder (horizontally opposed) diesel's direct driving carbon dioxide compressors. The latter part of the outward voyage was taken up with maintenance and proving that the dozens of brine circuits were leak-proof, and the multi-circuit cocks functioned correctly. Hand thermometer cords renewed where necessary and everything made ready for cooling down cargo spaces. The final discharge of general cargo took place in Townsville, Queensland and the loading of zinc and lead in the lower holds commenced.

One of the *Australia Star*'s public relations exercises was to invite the matron with some of her nurses from the local hospital to an evening dance with refreshments. The boat deck, under a canopy decorated with coloured lights provided a most suitable venue and the music being supplied by the

Australia Star

radiogram from the officers' lounge. On Friday, the day of the dance, the frig. department had commenced cooling down some of the spaces and eight-hour watches started. The chief was on 8–4, the third on the 8–12, and I was responsible for the 12–8 watch.

The dance was a very pleasant occasion and provided relaxation from watch-keeping and the monotony of shipboard life. The nurses also enjoyed the brief escape from similar working conditions: routine 24-hour duties under a demanding and responsible discipline, in their case providing succour and comfort to unfortunate members of the public.

I picked up my watch after the dance at midnight and after breakfast turned in knowing that we would be sailing at midnight. We would continue our loading at Port Alma (Rockhampton), Gladstone, Brisbane, Sydney, finally leaving Melbourne for a non-stop 30-day haul to the UK. The only break would be a few hours at anchor at St Vincent, Cape Verde Islands taking on fuel and water.

Two decks of chilled beef (29–30°F) were to be loaded at Melbourne to ascertain the practicability and economics of carrying meat in this way from Australia. A level between 9% and 12% of carbon dioxide was to be maintained in the gas-tight decks by injecting the gas through the fire extinguishing system with deck thermometer caps removed.

After a sound sleep and during 'tea and tab-nabs', I was considering whether to take advantage of a last chance to go ashore, when a colleague suggested I ring the nurse I had met at the dance. I took his advice and was invited to her home for dinner with her parents. Departing ship, anticipating a pleasant evening ashore, I failed to see on the gangway notice board that the ship's departure had been advanced one hour because loading had progressed better than expected. After driving some way out of Townsville along dark dirt roads, my taxi driver delivered me to a large wooden bungalow in the suburbs. There I was welcomed by my dancing

Townsville Custom House

partner and introduced to her family and my taxi was ordered to return for me at 11.00pm. A very pleasant evening was spent with the family; I suffered some anguish when the taxi failed to turn up on time, but after frantic phone calls arrived at 11.30pm. A hurried departure was made with a joking remark 'Hope you don't miss your ship!' The town traffic was negotiated with much skill by my driver and we arrived on the quay at ten minutes to midnight!

I was devastated to find a dimly lit dock with no ship! While I was collecting my shattered nerves a small boat tied up near me and its occupant told me he had just managed to get three crew members aboard the *Australia Star* when she dropped the docking pilot. They had also been caught out by the advanced sailing time, and I could see the departing lights of my ship out at sea. I was desolated by my predicament. What a contrast leaving a busy floodlight quay with winches working and the noise and bustle of loading to my quiet dark deserted dock with the knowledge of my ship ploughing her 16-knot furrow southwards. To cap it all, I had only three Australian pounds (30 shillings) in my pocket with which to catch her.

I was desperate to start the chase and asked my driver to take me to the nearest police station. We arrived there sometime after midnight and after a hurried explanation of my problem to the duty sergeant, I asked him for the BSL agent's telephone number so that I could obtain a ticket and hopefully catch a night mail train to Rockhampton. 'Hold on young Pommie' he said 'the next train to Rocky doesn't leave until 7.00pm this evening (Sunday), so the Dalgety agent won't be too pleased being woken up now! However, we can offer you a nice cell for the night, free, but would have to make a wee monetary charge for our padded cell. On the other hand you could have that free if we put you on a vagrancy charge!' My appreciation of his kind offer was blunted by the news of the delay in leaving Townsville. After establishing I had enough money to pay for my transport back to my dancing partner's bungalow, I told him I would take up his offer on my probable return.

It must have been well after 1.00am when I made a stealthy approach to the bungalow calling gently until my dancing partner was aroused and knew she had a shipless mariner on her hands! By now the family were awakened and kindly offered to put me up for the night, so I was able to pay off my patient taxi driver. They must experience many interesting aspects of life! Sunday would have been a very pleasant day if I had not had the constant worry of wondering if I could catch the *Australia Star* before she left Port Alma. The agent who had been contacted arranged to meet me with a rail ticket and pocket money, thought my ship would only be there a short time loading. The train travelling through the night and next day was scheduled to arrive at Rockhampton (300 miles) at three o'clock Monday afternoon.

Carnes Railway, Barron Falls

My DP's family's hospitality was wonderful, providing a bed on the veranda (the first and only time I have slept under a mosquito net), breakfast, lunch, etc. She was on day duty at the hospital, so I spent my time in the garden playing with her younger brother and sister. It was a relief, however, when I met the agent at the railway station and said farewell to my new found friends and was at last chasing the *Australia Star*.

The 20-hour journey will always be remembered by its contrast to my experience of rail travel in England where one could travel miles without speaking a word due to the reserved manner of the average Brit. Within ten minutes the occupants of my compartment (non-corridor) were introducing themselves and within an hour everyone was swapping yarns about their business and family life. My constant worry of catching my ship prevented me from enjoying to the full this unique way of travel. It was dark leaving Townsville and the night journey, along what I think was a single track with passing places, proceeded at what I imagined was 20-30 mph with frequent stops. There, all passengers including the train crew made a dash to corrugated iron huts with long bars on which awaited rows and rows of tea and coffee, but more prominent were pints of cool Fosters lager! Other comforts were attended to and after about 30 minutes the train crew would board, blowing the steam whistle for all passengers to embark. There was always some delay rounding up the Fosters enthusiasts!

The latter part of the journey in daylight, still proceeded at a slow pace but it gave me views of a very sparsely populated countryside, finally arriving at Rockhampton at about 3.00 pm. I bade farewell to my carriage companions who came from different walks of life, but were all 'cobbers at heart'. They wished me luck in the pursuit of my ship, but told me not to worry because if I failed, suggested that with my skills there was plenty of scope on sheep stations, maintaining engines, line shafting, etc. in the shearing sheds, or at cane sugar factories with their large boiling and crushing plants.

Fitzroy Bridge, Rockhampton

On enquiry I found the small train which served the Port Alma quay, some 15 miles down-river at its swampy estuary. It was a small wooden piled jetty and ships the size of the *Australia Star* had to be warped alongside with care because there was a danger of pulling the comparatively frail structure into the river. The train journey to the quay, which I thought was narrow gauge, was unique, I in a small caboose behind wagons loaded with frozen meat and bales of wool. Imagine my relief when I discovered that this was the last consignment before the *Australia Star* sailed.

My ETA had obviously proceeded me, because as I approached the ship a group of officers, on the lookout greeted me with a cheer. I was welcomed aboard with proclamations 'the chief engineer of the *Marie Celeste* has arrived' and 'here comes the Ancient Mariner'. One colleague imitated a news reporter with pad 'Tell us sir about your "walk-about" in the wilds of Townsville's outback?'

This jocular reception was lost on me, because having caught my ship I now had to face up to the trouble my misdemeanour had caused, another engineer having to carry out my duties, etc., so I was bracing myself for the reprimands awaiting me from Mr Brady and our chief Mr Slessor. When I found Mr Brady in the brine-room, he was obviously pleased to see me, but only had time to tell me to report to Mr Slessor. He listened to my story patiently and took me to task over my careless, irresponsible conduct, but I think realised my mistake was a genuine one and pointed out the worry it had caused, especially if I had missed the ship at Port Alma as the duties on the freezer were at their busiest; preparing for the loading of apples, eggs, cheese, frozen beef, lamb, and crates of rabbit carcasses complete with fur. I think he also knew I had suffered during my 'French leave' and instructed me to return in my number one rig and accompany him to the skipper. As he dismissed me he looked up from his desk with a twinkle in his eye and asked 'was she worth it?'.

My dressing down before Captain Fisher in the presence of Mr Slessor was daunting and resulted in two days' pay plus travelling expenses being deducted from my salary. That was my first and only misdemeanour during my twelve years at sea and henceforth departure boards were always given special attention!

On arrival in London we learnt that our ship was to make a similar voyage terminating again at Townsville. While on a few days' leave and knowing that Staffordshire pottery was approved worldwide, I purchased a Royal Doulton dinner service, a doll for my DP's sister and an English football for her brother who had only seen rugby balls which apparently was the only game played. The presents were destined for my Australian hosts in appreciation of their spontaneous hospitality given to a young Englishman adrift 'down-under'.

Unfortunately, 'Murphy's Law' intervened, when the voyage (October – January 1938) terminated at Brisbane.

After considerable difficulty in arranging customs' clearance, etc. the presents were posted to Townsville but I never heard whether my hosts received them nor did I return there again even though I made further trips to Australia during the War in the *Sydney Star*, *Imperial Star*, *Royal Star* and *Empire Might*.

Chapter Five

SAILING INTO CONFLICT

IN June 1939 I embarked on the *Fresno Star* for my second voyage to the North Pacific coast of North America via the Panama Canal. We left North Shields on 13 June 1939 settling down to the business of getting her to the ports of call on schedule, not an easy task because she was an old-time coal burner. Fortunately the majority of the engineer officers were experienced in coal firing and sailing from the Tyne provided, in the main, an experienced crew of coal firemen.

ss Fresno Star

Our passage outwards followed the normal pattern, topping up coal bunkers at Port Royal (Kingston), Jamaica, but unfortunately at Panama Canal a snag occurred. An elderly lady en route to Vancouver was occupying the only spare cabin in the officers' accommodation. Canal dues were governed by cubic capacity, type of cargo or service; passenger ships incurred much higher rates and because the *Fresno Star* was carrying one passenger the authorities were claiming the higher dues. The cost difference must have been considerable because Captain Palmer with the concurrence of the agents had no alternative but to arrange the disembarkation of the frail old lady, including her baggage, from our anchorage during the early hours of the morning. We were very upset seeing the lady being put to such inconvenience; for a younger person it could have been an adventure - a train journey through the Canal Zone with overnight accommodation at Panama City would have been interesting.

After picking up our transhipped passenger we continued our voyage to Vancouver calling at San Pedro and San Francisco. On my first trip at San Pedro I was able to visit Los Angeles. Hollywood then was the world centre of the film industry; Sunset Boulevard, Beverley Hills were explored with wonderment and it was an experience to have seen the famous Chinese Threatre and Brown Derby which many film stars frequented. On the same trip at San Francisco I managed to see *Gone with the Wind* on its first showing, it being the forerunner of the epic films and I think the first where, because of its length, an interval was needed.

New Westminster, our terminal port, gave me the impression that we had arrived in China not Canada, because Chinese shops and businesses dominated the dock area. I was able to make a number of sight-seeing visits to Vancouver, the most memorable being on an old tramcar which had been converted into an observation car. I understood that the chassis was one of the original bogies first used on British Columbia Electric Railway Company's network. It was the perfect way to tour the city with two well-known men, driver and conductor the latter character, Teddy Lyons, whose commentary was not only informative but first-class comedy. I remember in one of the quiet suburban streets we stopped and Teddy attracted birds which fed from his hands. Apparently they never failed to turn up for their regular tit-bits.

All aboard the BC tramcar, July 1939. SWS 2nd from left

Homeward bound we sailed into Puget Sound calling at Tacoma and Seattle. The Tacoma Narrows' suspension bridge was of graceful construction and for me a novel experience to walk over; in those days bridges built by this method were unique. Little did I realise that it would suffer a catastrophic failure a year later. It was claimed to be the third longest suspension bridge in the USA. The centre span of 2800 feet was supported by towers 425 feet high, designed to allow movement at the top of up to five feet in either direction and movement could be felt when walking over, even in the mildest breezes, increasing quite dramatically in strong winds.

The bridge was known locally as 'Galloping Gertie' and motorists felt rather uncomfortable negotiating the rolling and rippling roadway in breezy weather. Engineers tried various methods to stop the motion of the bridge, including extra cables, but on the morning of 7 November 1940 the deck started moving in a steady vertical oscillation. The bridge had been designed to withstand winds never recorded on Puget Sound - gusts of up to 122 mph - but in fact started 'galloping' when gusts of only 35 mph hit it, from the side.

At 10.00am the concerned highways department closed the bridge to traffic and with winds topping 40 mph the deck of the bridge began to twist wildly from side to side. At 11 o'clock a 600-foot length of the main span tore loose from the suspenders and plunged into the swift, cold waters 190 feet below. The entire disaster was filmed (I saw it in England on the *Movetone News*) and stunned bridge engineers were able to study the momentous collapse. It was concluded that the combination of solid web-plate girders with a solid floor, which prevented the passage of even low velocity winds, together with the high flexibility of the structure, made the bridge susceptible to vertical undulations which tended to change into twisting motions. A replacement did not open until 1950 and was built thicker and wider, using deeper truss-like girders which allowed the winds to pass through.

It transpired that timber in its various forms was the cargo to be shipped from this area. No wonder, wood was to be seen everywhere, many saw-mills, mountains of sawdust and all the houses built of wood with fire-hydrants every hundred yards.

Mid-centenary celebrations were taking place during our visit to mark the occasion when the State of Washington joined the Union (42nd State, 11 November 1889). I was impressed with the noisy razzmatazz in which the inhabitants enjoyed themselves, particularly the way the huge cars were driven with hooters blowing, accompanied with minor explosions from their exhausts. On investigation I found that a spark lead had been removed from the engine and reconnected to a plug fitted into the exhaust pipe. I saw one tail pipe depart from the car with a terrific clatter, and learned that the guy who created the loudest explosion became 'Top of the Bangs'.

At an air display during the celebrations I was able to make my first flight in a 'covered in' monoplane. Previous occasions had been in open cockpit biplanes. At the tender age of five or six my father persuaded Alan Cobham (later to be knighted), to take me and my pal (probably against regulations) for a flip over Bradwell Wood near Burslem. I do remember the landing because my cheek bumped on the leather cockpit surround making me cry. Father was in real trouble when mother found out - subjecting her child to such danger. Later joy rides, when a teenager, were made at Rhyl - take off and landing from the sands when the tide was out 17/6d (85p) a flip.

The monoplane at Tacoma was a four-seater with dual controls. I was in the front with the pilot with two shipmates behind. On request I was allowed, under instructions, to fly the plane for a few minutes, much to the anxiety of my brother officers!

Our next port of call was Portland, Oregon, which required a long pilotage in the Columbia River. Stand-by in the engine-room, in addition to normal watches, limited observation of river passages, but I do remember with pleasure the overpowering, refreshing smell of the pine woods flowing down the engine and stokehold ventilators; it compensated for our confinement in the steamy, noisy mechanical environment. I was fortunate in being able to obtain glimpses of the beautiful pine covered hills during the latter part of the passage.

After a short stay at Portland we proceeded to San Francisco for our final cargo. I was able to exchange my Emerson radio for a similar model but with an ultra short-wave band enabling me to receive BBC news programmes. 'Frisco Paddy' exhanged my wireless set. He was known worldwide for his business deals with seafarers, reputed to be able to exchange, sell and deliver on board anything that was available in San Francisco provided it was transportable.

The set I had bought at Liverpool before we left was useless at sea unable to receive foreign broadcasts. The new radio was to play an important part later; already the news from home was worrying.

During our short stay we were able to visit Treasure Island to see the Golden Gate International Exposition - a complementary one was also held in New York. Its grandeur and unique shows from different countries were very exciting. Two items, I remember, were to see tiny babies being kept in incubators; they must have been the forerunners of modern equipment used for premature babies. Nearby was Sally Rand's Nude Ranch - again a forerunner of things to come! As we left San Francisco we sailed past the infamous Alcatraz Federal US Prison - a forbidding place, particularly with the knowledge that it contained at that time many notorious criminals.

We were on our final leg to Panama, South of San Pedro, when one of our firemen developed symptoms of appendicitis which had been diagnosed from numerous wireless messages between our second officer and doctors in a British-American company's plantation; I think it was in Guatemala. For two days our crew member's condition was monitored, but when the symptoms showed a worsening condition, they indicated an operation was urgent. The nearest anchorage, where arrangements could be made to collect the patient and transport him to the company's hospital miles inland, was some 300 miles south of our current position. Our average speed was 10-11 knots.

There was no need to convey to the ship's company that getting the *Fresno* to the anchorage as quickly as possible was of paramount importance in saving the life of our crew member. My first indication that the ship's speed was going to be increased was when the normal 12-4 was accompanied with the 4-8 firemen and trimmers, with a request to double-bank the boilers. The problem of getting sufficient steam to maintain normal service speed disappeared immediately! By the time I returned below to relieve the 'third', engine revolutions had already increased; he had opened the HP expansions to accommodate the increased steam flow and departed for his lunch with instructions to open up further if necessary.

The next 24 hours was an experience to be remembered in the engine room and stokehold. I wondered whether the old *Fresno* had ever gone so fast in her life, an average speed of 13+ knots was maintained, not bad for a 20 year-old ship. One fireman working two fires instead of four made a big difference to the boilers' output, the problem being in the engine room accepting the increased steam flow without lifting the safety valves. Coping with higher than normal revolutions on the main engines and auxiliaries brought out the skills of the double-banked greasers. Oiling the twin triple expansion engines was by hand-feeding the oil into cups on the crossheads, normally a skilful job, but at the increased revs, greater accuracy and timing were needed. Certain crosshead guides needed special attention because of overheating, depending on the list of the ship, which was always difficult to keep on an even keel. When the port or starboard engine showed its displeasure, small balls of oily tallow were thrown by the greasers on to the affected guide. This entailed split-second timing in order to hit the target and soothe the hot shining surfaces and miss the rapidly moving crossheads, otherwise it was thrown back into their faces.

All this action was maintained under tropical conditions, giving a smooth passage but the humidity and temperature conditions down below were very uncomfortable. High sea water termperature reduced its cooling effect on all systems decreasing condenser vacuum with resultant loss of main engine efficiency. Also a maximum demand was required for the refrigeration compressors working at full power to maintain below freezing temperatures in the cargo spaces surrounded by warm sea and air. Above in my cabin the normal subdued noise and vibration levels were increased to such an extent that I had to wedge my water decanter and glasses to stop them rattling so I could get some sleep.

We reached our rendezvous hours ahead of the first radioed ETA but a launch was waiting to pick up our patient who was rushed away, with shouts of 'Good luck, see you on the Tyne, Hinny'. We heard later that a successful operation led to his recovery. Little did we realise that the spontaneous united efforts of our crew to help a person in danger was a foretaste of the national effort by the British and other nationals during the next few years.

Our passage to and through the Panama was completed by the end of August and we were put to an anchorage awaiting sailing orders. In the meantime, the *Fresno* was painted overall grey obliterating the distinctive Blue Star Line's colours. We sailed for home on 3 September and the next night after I had completed my watch at midnight, I tuned in to the BBC on my new radio and heard the disconcerting news that the *Athenia* had been torpedoed.

The following 12-days passage home was mentally horrendous. We down below the water line were conscious of sound transmission through water. How I wished I had adjusted that port main engine bottom end bearing a little tighter to reduce its thumping. On the other hand it would then have presented a real problem of everheating during our emergency high-speed run to save our appendicitis patient.

There we were pounding along between 10 and 12 knots knowing that our faithful reciprocating engines were broadcasting our presence to the U-boats which were sinking ships all around us. Little comfort was gained knowing that our only armament was a revolver and rifle kept by the 'old man' in case of mutiny!

A large tanker a few hours ahead of us, on the same course, was sunk. Later that night as we passed near her last radioed position we could smell the fuel oil all around us.

We were lucky we arrived safely at Liverpool on 15 September 1939. We had sailed in peace and returned to Europe at war . . . for a time called the 'Phoney War' but at sea for the Merchant Navy and Royal Navy a real one.

I left the *Fresno Star* as I had spent sufficient time on deep-sea articles to study and sit for my second's ticket (Ministry of Transport Second Class Engineer).

Chapter Six

A Spell Ashore

THERE were no marine colleges in Staffordshire where I could attend, in order to supplement the technical knowledge already gained at sea with many hours of maintenance and operational responsibilities, before sitting for the Ministry of Transport's examination. The certificate of competency (in my case, as second class engineer in steamships) comprised papers on strength of materials, shipbuilding, heat engines, electricity, and questions on the operation and maintenance of steam turbines, reciprocating engines, condensers, auxiliaries and boilers. The longest paper was machine drawing, a candidate was allowed from 10.00am to 4.00pm to complete with no break. Sandwiches were allowed and visits to the toilet were accompanied by the examiner's clerk to ensure that no design formula was acquired in order to produce a working drawing of the component requested in the question.

Later, when the written examination papers had been marked an interview was arranged during which the examiner would orally question the candidate. The period could vary from twenty minutes to an hour, when he may first ask the candidate to elaborate on some of the answers on his written work, and then ask questions to test his engineering knowledge. An example could be to describe the duties of the responsible engineer before, during and after a ship was dry-docked. The answers ranging from what action was necessary to ensure the ship was stable and on an even keel before entering, shutting down progressively the auxiliary machinery before the loss of cooling water and then, in conjunction with the dock management providing adequate electrical, water supplies, etc. for the ship's and shore staff to carry out their respective duties. During the stay in dry dock to agree the extent of maintenance on hull, valve injections, tail-end, propellers, rudder and work on internal machinery, afterwards; to inspect and ensure the repairs were to specification. Finally, responsible that all areas where work on hull and connections to it were watertight also the ship would be in a stable condition before refloating commenced and raising steam to re-establish the operation of the ship's auxiliary plant. The oral examination could fail a candidate even when his written papers were satisfactory, it ensured that the candidate was practically competent in the true sense of the word.

I decided to attend the London County Council's College of Navigation and Marine Engineering in Poplar High Street, East London, and because it was within walking distance, to stay at the British Sailors Society's headquarters office on the corner of East and West India Dock roads. There were a number of small rooms available for officers to stay while studying for their tickets, with the use of the office staff canteen and a labour exchange nearby. Before my time, an officer had to provide his wherewithal and received no salary while he was ashore studying to sit for his ticket. I had the advantage of collecting unemployment benefit (dole, 30/ - a week), and by special arrangement, required to sign on before school on Monday morning with the privilege of not being offered work that week! The money did help with my expenses but with no salary the drain on my finances was an encouraging factor for conscientious study and to 'sit' for the examination as soon as possible.

It was coincidental that I had been shown this area when a young teenager by my father, I vividly remember China Town and he obtaining permission for me to go inside Charley Brown's public house, in order to see behind the bar, dozens of curios from all parts of the world, obtained from sailors in exchange for drink. My time at school passed quickly, there was little room for anything else, but some relief was obtained by visits to Petticoat Lane on Sunday mornings. It provided a very interesting couple of hours but one had to be there early, before 8.00am, to see the action. The variety of stalls and the cosmopolitan crowds made a colourful scene with the cries and antics of the traders making first-class entertainment. It was reputed that an item could be stolen at one end and sold at the other. My observations confirmed that this could easily occur in the crush of people in the narrow street with stalls on each side.

Due to the 'black out' travelling any distance was inconvenient particularly for strangers so the odd Saturday night's visit to the 'S–s Opera', in Poplar provided some bawdy entertainment, I can't remember the theatre's proper name. There was a bar with a glass partition at the side of the auditorium which enabled drinkers to watch the show, without interruption and keep their glasses filled! Much of the entertainment came

Mr Lundberg in Burslem Park

from that quarter especially when a turn met with their disapproval, whereupon, sometimes the bar 'hangers on' would mount the stage and give their version on how it should be done. I'm sure any turn which could satisfy the audiences in that theatre would be able to withstand any amount of abuse from audiences in any part of the country.

I obtained my second's ticket just before Christmas. To receive the examiner's handshake with his congratulations, gave one a wonderful sense of achievement, instead of he recommending my return to sea for six months before attempting to retake the examination. In a very happy frame of mind I travelled home to celebrate, taking with me Mr Lundberg who had also passed the same examination. He was a Dutch engineer from the Straits Steamship Company, Singapore, who had found the time, in London digs, very lonely during his two months' stay, so I had invited him to my home to see what the provinces could do! People in 'The Potteries' during the early part of the war had little personal contact with foreigners; so he enjoyed the small town hospitality and proved most interesting to my friends, particularly as he was able to describe with photographs, what life was like in the Far East and soon acquired the affectionate nickname 'Dutchie'. He also had to report weekly with his passport, to the Burslem police station, a war-time security requirement.

In the early days of the war Merchant Navy personnel when ashore, wore civilian clothes but later uniform was used. One of the main reasons was we had to use our civilian 'clothes coupons' to renew our uniforms, etc, as the allowances did not allow us to buy additional gear. In addition later on, the few places for relaxation, mainly in HM forces' establishments, required the wearing of uniforms and entrance fees reduced to some cinemas and places of entertainment. Later, however, there was such a huge variety of uniformed men when other nations entered the conflict, it became very confusing for some of the older civilians; I recall on a number of occasions being offered the fare by dear old ladies when entering a bus.

I'm sure when Mr Lundberg left after Christmas he had a better appreciation of the British people but unfortunately it was marred by an unpleasant incident. On the Saturday night before his return to London, he was involved in a small fracas with a British soldier. A group of us had spent a very pleasant evening at a dance and were chatting outside in the black-out before dispersing to go our different ways home. Suddenly I heard raised voices caused by a soldier pushing Dutchie against the building, fortunately I with the help of his two companions were able to separate them before the fisticuffs started to fly. It transpired that one of our girls, a previous acquaintance of the soldier, called out, bidding him good night and he was obviously annoyed that she had a new escort, a 'B— civilian to boot!' The soldier was 'half-seas over' and his companions had difficulty in frog marching him away. I was furious and decided some retribution was required, unfortunately the girl did not know his name, only knew he was a sergeant and that his contingent was billeted in a school, in Hanley, during the Christmas holidays.

After Mr Lundberg's departure I donned my uniform, found the school and after a 'butt salute' was escorted to a major, the commanding officer.

After explaining the reason for my visit he apologised for the sergeant's behaviour and said he would like to discipline his man provided I could identify him, explaining there were five sergeants in his unit. No way could I recognise him because it all happened in complete darkness but I thought I could distinctly remember his voice. He agreed to interview them individually in my presence. I identified the third man as the culprit who, with no hesitation confirmed that he had had an argument with some civies with his lady friend. A genuine apology was made when he knew he had insulted a foreign merchant man who had already experienced running through the U-boat gauntlet sailing into Britain. The Major then invited me and Mr Lundberg to a dance arranged for the following weekend at the school, when an apology would be made to Mr Lundberg and the drinks, etc, would be 'on' his unit. Unfortunately Dutchie could not return but I was able to convey the appropriate apology to him for the Army's misdemeanour and attended the dance with my friends which proved to be a pleasant occasion. The sergeant was a reasonable man and like many young men including myself at that time, were aware that their future may be short-lived; in addition in his case he was harassed by the influx of many raw recruits. Understandably, nervous tensions already strained only required a minor upset to cause an aggressive outburst.

At that time it was possible to sit for part A of the first class certificate before going to sea again to serve the required sea service for the full examination. As I was in an academic frame of mind, I decided to return to school in London to sit for this examination. In late January during a weekend's visit home, when answering the door, there standing before me in baggy trousers, old woollen jersey and small suitcase, looking very forlorn, was Mr Lundberg! He had been torpedoed in a Blue Funnel ship which was lost off the Spanish coast when working his passage home to Singapore. He had lost all his possessions including two expensive cameras with much equipment (he was an enthusiastic photographer) and spent two days in atrocious weather in a lifeboat before being rescued and landed at Gibraltar. After staying at my home for a few days he returned to Liverpool, eventually sailing homewards. Later during my war service I tried to get in touch with him writing to his forwarding address at The Institute of Marine Engineers Singapore, but was unsuccessful.

Unfortunately, during February, my father died suddenly and, as the eldest son, I went home to make the funeral arrangements for my invalid mother, afterwards returning to sea to support her and my two younger brothers. After the burial I voiced my doubts to the funeral director that I thought he had been buried in the wrong grave. A hurried check through the records with the vicar, proved my suspicion to be correct. My parents had bought a grave for my elder brother who had died as a few months old baby. At the time a glass dome with artificial flowers identified its position, but over the years it had been damaged, removed and the grave became overgrown. The vicar and undertaker were very concerned and apologetic and said they would make arrangements for the coffin to be transferred. Fortunately, my mother was unable to attend the funeral being confined to her bed, otherwise she would have been most upset, knowing intimately the grave site. Permission had to be obtained from the Home Office for the exhumation of my father's coffin, requiring my signature on official forms, etc, posted to my home during my return to Blue Star Line duties, which aroused my mother's suspicions that something was wrong. My brothers and I had kept the mistake secret from her for obvious reasons making it a worrying time for all of us. However, two weeks later it was arranged for the exhumation to take place at dawn, witnessed by me, a Home Office representative, the police, vicar and undertaker on a bitter wintry morning with inches of snow on the ground. I had also arranged the transfer of the wreaths so that, later in the afternoon, I could show my mother the grave. I shall always remember carrying her, wrapped in blankets, to the grave because the car could not negotiate the ice and snow to the site. During the minutes spent at the grave the sun lit up the scene and thankfully my brothers and I saw that our mother was at last contented and satisfied that father was at rest.

Little did I realise that she would die later that year when I was the other side of the world during my second voyage on the *Sydney Star*.

After my father's death and on my return to the Blue Star Line, I was appointed to sea-going duties as junior third engineer on the *Sydney Star*.

We had left Liverpool August 1940 with four other merchantmen taking urgently required reinforcements to Egypt; the *Sydney* was the slowest ship (17 knots) and we carried light tanks, tracked personnel carriers, ammunitions, bombs, petrol and much equipment for the forces who were carried on a troop ship (I think an Empress liner). It was the only time that I was to sail in such a large Royal Naval convoy. We were surrounded by aircraft-carriers, battleships with supporting cruisers, destroyers, etc, and it proved to be a demanding time in the engine room maintaining maximum knots, with frequent signals to try and increase speed.

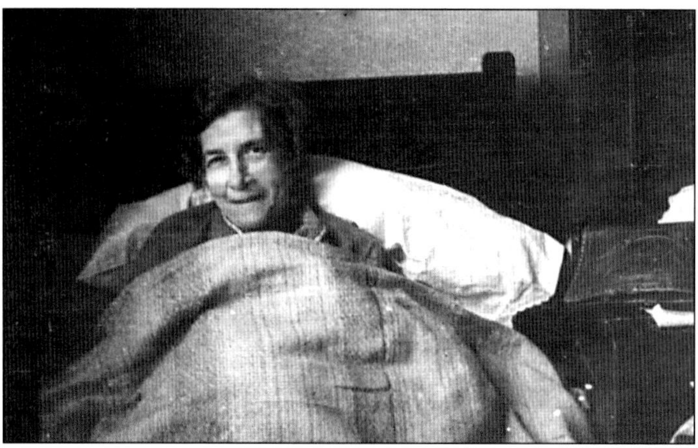

My mother

The large Naval force left the convoy when West of Gibraltar obviously bound for the Mediterranean, leaving us with the troopship, supply vessels and *HMS Argus* an old aircraft-carrier; she was to leave later at a latitude near Sierra Leone, and was carrying fighter planes which would be landed and flown across Africa to the war zones in the desert.

Our Naval escort which included *HMS Kelly* continued to guard the convoy, with brief stops at Cape Town and Durban for fuel, water and provisions. We arrived at Port Said after a very exacting time in the engine room, keeping the twin Burmeister & Wain main engines at full power and when sea water temperatures allowed, a high percentage of overload. Shortly after our arrival we were requested to parade in 'number one uniform', on the boat-deck, where an admiral complimented the ship's company for their contribution towards carrying much needed reinforcements quickly on the long voyage round South Africa. Shortly after our departure, enroute for Bombay, we heard that *HMS Kelly* had been in action in the Mediterranean.

Bombay gave me my first glimpse of India, an outstanding education for me. It was unique to see at the cinema some gentlemen escorting two or three wives, the youngest with a baby, all beautifully dressed and obviously enjoying the evening entertainment. And where members of our crew on the quay, had a monetary/cruelty disagreement with a Garry-Wallah, removed the horse (bag of bones) trotted it onboard, hauled the gangway inboard and turned in. Much later the mate organised the 'nag's' return to the owner having benefited from its best feed for years from the galley scraps!

From Bombay we sailed to Australia for food supplies where on arrival in Sydney, I received a cable informing me of my mother's death two days previously.

My father left, cruising on the Esperance Bay *with a crew member 1936*

Chapter Seven

THE MISSING SWASTIKA

THE voyage of the *mv Sydney Star* to New Zealand via the Panama Canal started on a cold miserable day in April 1940. She had been fitted with machine gun nests on the bridge and boat deck, but there had been insufficient time to install the mounting to carry the Lewis guns.

In those early days of the War there were no Royal Navy personnel, later called DEMS, to man the armaments on Merchant Navy ships. Before we sailed all the officers and some of the men were given a very brief period of instruction on how to load and to free the mechanism of the guns if they jammed; apparently a frequent occurrence. Later our skipper, Captain TS Horn, arranged a roster so that 'all hands and the cook' took turns in the gun-nests defending our ship against possible air attack.

I forget the number of two-hour watches, in addition to my normal duties, I spent in those cold concrete lined tubs, perched high up to give a good view, which ensured they were well exposed to the weather. How grateful we were to those ladies who had knitted the woollen comforts for the forces, boxes of which had been handed over to us just before we sailed. The Balaclavas were a godsend on those cold gun watches and at least they made us look hostile; just like Bairnsfather's 'Old Bill', in my case minus a moustache.

The Lewis guns when loaded were heavy so we rested them on the parapet, but with no guide rails. I'm sure we were lucky that no attack materialised before we got out of range of the Luftwaffe, because none of the guns had been fired by us. Goodness knows how we would have controlled them, manhandling them with no support! I reckon we would have caused more damage to ourselves, with no limiting guard rail - my colleague or myself on the opposite side of the boat deck, in the excitement following a moving target, could have shot ourselves to pieces including the funnel.

Our voyage, blacked-out and unescorted to the Panama was uneventful - thank goodness! Also our passage in the Pacific (with no black-out) to New Zealand and return to the Panama Canal. However, it was while we were passing through the Gaillard-Cut that the *Sydney* hit some obstruction, causing damage for'd with leakage in the fore peak area making it necessary to carry out temporary repairs. This caused an unscheduled stop, for two days, at Colon: replacement of rivets and a concrete box built internally around the leaking area.

At that time the USA had not entered the war, therefore the Canal Zone was neutral territory and Germany had an embassy there. After the first night's shore leave and early the following morning, we on board found that a British Expeditionary Force had been active. In the accommodation aft. were stowed, a German flag and a large plaque. There seemed to be an air of jubilation among the crew and local stevedores over the acquisition

Gaillard-Cut

of the obviously stolen items. It later transpired that our two cadets were responsible for stealing the flag and embassy nameplate during the early hours.

Apparently, the intrepid pair had climbed up on to the second-storey balcony and taken the flag while the ambassador slept, snores could be heard through an adjacent jalousie. At street level they had laboriously scraped and chipped away the plaque's fastenings in the concrete wall, a difficult and laborious job made even longer by the necessity of keeping noise level to a minimum, and requiring two men to lift the cast-brass plaque. The Italian ambassador in the embassy opposite was awakened by cheers and laughter from the morning passers-by and it was he who notified the German ambassador that some of his possessions were adrift. It was reported that the German ambassador's display of rage on the balcony on seeing his loss considerably increased the amusement of the assembled crowd.

On board, our two cadets must have suffered the displeasure of the skipper and chief officer for their enterprise. Identification of the wrong-doers was not difficult as ours was the only British ship in Colon at the time. Later during the afternoon, our boys had to appear with the evidence at a court of law to answer the charges of stealing German property. We were told they were the most popular thieves that had appeared in court for some time, but the dignity of the court was maintained, and fines were imposed after a severe dressing down by the magistrate. I cannot remember what the fines were but they must have been a considerable worry to our young men. To the joy of everyone aware of the case, particularly the cadets, the fines were paid by the Blue Star Line agents, who in addition sent to the *Sydney Star* two barrels of beer for the crew to celebrate the release and return of the prisoners!

mv Sydney Star

We departed the Canal Zone in good spirits having been given a moral boost to the serious business of making the unescorted passage home, the deck officers to navigate and maintain a constant vigilance. The engine room staff, below sea level, ensuring that the huge, noisy, smelly Burmeister & Wain double-acting two-stroke diesels, kept pounding the slightly crumpled bow on a zig-zag course to blacked-out UK.

There was no doubt a certain German ambassador would have given the *Sydney Star*'s departure time, and ETA North Atlantic, etc, to Berlin, with a special request to arrange the delivery of a tin fish, with his initials on it, to prevent our arrival in the UK, even though he had his flag and plaque returned!

We arrived safely at Liverpool 28 July 1940.

I wondered whether those two cadets survived the War and became master mariners? They certainly had the qualities of drive, courage and leadership, provided it was directed into the right channels!

After a short leave I was requested to transfer to the *mv Imperial Star* which made an unescorted four-months' voyage via South Africa discharging war supplies and then on to New Zealand for food.

The ports of Cape Town and Port Elizabeth were becoming familiar to me but Hobart, Tasmania and Bluff on the southern coast of New Zealand's South Island were new venues. Hobart was a short stay loading food but I remember we tied up alongside the large IXL fruit canning factory, well known to me as a child from the delicious tinned fruits I had enjoyed.

mv Imperial Star

Bluff was only a small, mainly fishing, port but was the export point for the frozen lamb, etc, from the southern area. It was also known to seafarers as a 'dry port', no alcoholic drink available and I believe this sobering feature extended as far inland as Invercargill! The people of Bluff made us very welcome during the few days we were there; impromptu dances were arranged in the one and only church hall and groups of crew members invited to parties in their homes. The food: the home cooking was wonderful and Blue-Point oysters in so many dishes, I'm not sure but I think they were incorporated into some confectionery recipes! Apparently our visit enabled the refrigeration works to recommence production after many weeks shut-down, due to the storage rooms being full because the war had seriously curtailed the arrival of refrigerator ships.

We departed with a sense of well being knowing that we had helped a very caring and most hospitable community with, I well remember, the odd tearful eye on our departure and their good wishes for our safe return to the UK to deliver their contribution to the war effort.

Our final loading port was Napier, in the past subjected to earthquakes, after which we would start our unescorted, zig-zag, submarine dodging course for blacked-out Britain via the Panama Canal.

At Napier the *Imperial Star* had to anchor awaiting a berth. It was a beautiful day but a large swell in the bay was causing the ship to roll heavily. As junior third engineer I was off watch enjoying the pleasant Sunday afternoon when the second engineer approached seeking a volunteer to examine the ship's siren (operated on compressed air) which had ceased to function. He explained that the chief electrician had reported the electrical solenoid functioned because it could be heard operating from deck-level. The second, further explained that he did not want to send an assistant engineer to examine the siren which was positioned many feet above the crows nest with no access platform and he preferred a certified engineer to carry out the job.

I donned a boiler suit and climbed the mast to see what tools I would need. An iron ladder terminated just below the huge horn and the feeling in my stomach made me aware that a considerable movement was taking place, which was confirmed when I looked skyward or down to the deck. I realised that I was on a gyrating elliptical course which varied to break the monotony!

Descending with some relief, but now knowing what I had let myself in for, I returned with a bag of tools which I attached to the rungs of the ladder below the horn and by its pendulum movement it gave a local indication that my work place was unstable. Requiring both hands to work, I threaded one of my legs through the ladder rungs and started to chip away layers of paint from the nuts and inspection cover, silently blessing the over enthusiasm of the many deck-hands who had painted them from a bosun's chair, suitably lashed to the mast.

After about twenty minutes' work I was rewarded: with the cover removed I could see that a circle of rubber insertion joint was jamming the operating piston. From my lofty uncomfortable perch I silently blessed the unmarried gentleman's son who had some time previously remade a pipe joint, most probably in the engine room, when the knocked-out centre piece of jointing had fallen into the pipe system and failed to retrieve it, eventually finishing up at the end of the line. After further work I was able to remove the obstruction and boxed up the valve-body.

The second mate, who had occasionally been observing my activities through a telescope, originally called out, 'had I permission to be up his mast?' and later if I felt sick, to use my tool-bag as the mate would not want his mast soiled! I now instructed him to try the siren.

We were both rewarded with a long blast which was deafening to me, even with my ears finger-plugged and was surprised by the resultant level of vibration of the mast and my ladder! However, I indicated to him to give the siren another blast to ensure it was working satisfactorily. He must have been a man with a musical flair, because he then proceeded to give a rendering of what I thought was the last bars of the well-known tune *Colonel Bogey*, which was confirmed by me because the vibrating ladder gave me a funny feeling in my groin!

Suddenly, we both received a blast from another direction, it was the 'old man' bellowing from the bridge, 'what the b--- did we both think we were doing?' Amongst other things, we must have awoken him from his siesta. I decided it was time to retreat, with my bag of tools, deckwards, noting that the second mate was being given a barrage of Murphy's compliments!

The blasts had reverberated around the bay echoing from the cliffs, there was no need for me to acquaint the second engineer that all was well because the whole ship's company was wondering what was going on and I thought most of the shore-side wallahs too, with some of them looking seawards to see what all the hooting was about!

Later I indicated to the second that I now appreciated why he wanted a 'certified' engineer to do the job! I also sympathised with the second mate when he recounted his upbraiding from Captain Miller who told him that the signal he had sounded was an urgent request for a doctor and ambulance launch to be dispatched to the ship. Fortunately, no action materialised, most probably because the port authorities were confused and seeing no ship on fire or sinking, awaited a repeat signal. I consoled him with the thought, that if a doctor had come out, his trip would not have been fruitless, at least he could have examined my head!

We both agreed that it was typical of the seafaring life that one could not expect a compliment every time a job was successfully completed!

Our voyage across the Pacific Ocean and through the Panama Canal passed without incident. However, I think it was the *Imperial* but may have been the *Sydney* when within two days' sailing distance to the UK and during a game of deck tennis, with life-jackets to hand, we spotted a plane making an approach. Assuming it was one of ours we started to wave a welcome which was short-lived because it began to strafe our ship! My colleagues near to a companion ladder slid down and disappeared into the accommodation and I dived under a spare propeller which was carried on the boat deck. The plane returned sweeping down the port side firing its machine guns and then made off. Fortunately no one was hurt and little damage done.

We arrived safely in Liverpool August 1941 and I left the *Imperial Star*.

However, she was lost on her next voyage in a Malta convoy being torpedoed in the stern losing rudder and both propellers. Valiant attempts by the Royal Navy to tow her failed and after taking off all personnel was sunk with depth charges.

The *Sydney Star* was also torpedoed in the same convoy but managed to limp into Malta with her desperately needed supplies. She also suffered many air raids during her four months' stay whilst being repaired. She survived the war.

Chapter Eight

A U-Boat Leads the Convoy

I WAS third engineer officer on the *ss Royal Star*, one of the 'Old Battle Squadron' built at the end of the First World War. My cabin was austere but it did have the luxury of a 'bulkhead dynamo', and was on the port side; its door opened on to an outboard open companionway, exposed to the prevailing weather. Ideal when fine but often in rough conditions, due to a leaking door, awash with inches of sea water slopping about the deck. It was not uncommon to have my seaboots adjacent to my bunk ready to slip into so that I could complete my ablutions in cold water at the 'compactum'. At night one had to listen to the seas coming inboard in order to time one's exit, making a mad dash along the deck between waves of sea water going in the same direction. During the day, by observing the sea conditions through a small porthole, a more successful passage was made aft to the engine room entrance - the wetness factor was improved.

The advent of the magnetic mine during the early part of the War caused the loss of many ships until the system of degaussing was fitted. Degaussing Gear (DG) as it was called neutralised the magnetic property of the steel ship by passing electrical energy through huge coils installed around the hull of the ship.

The DG had been hastily fitted prior to my first voyage (18 October 1941) from the Royal Victoria Docks London to Australia via South Africa and returning via Cape Town. Before we left, the ship was 'wiped' (presumably to neutralise residual longitudinal magnetism which I understood was worked into ships when being built in the stocks), by energising two large cables which were passed under the keel encircling the hull, one for'd and one aft of the midships section. I understood a high voltage 'flash' technique was used.

The main DG coil comprised a continuously-laid cable, in the scuppers on the main outside deck, running completely round the ship many times fore and aft thus forming a huge electro-magnet and was energised by direct current (DC) from a 110V-dynamo. One could not think of a more unsuitable place to put electric cables, being continuously engulfed in salt water in rough weather and baked hot through the tropics. However, it was essential that some form of protection be fitted to all ships as quickly as possible. One of three, single-cylinder steam-driven dynamos supplied the current and the flux-density (magnetism) was varied by a series of knife switches in the dynamo flat which reduced or increased the number of coils energised.

Magnetism was reduced sailing southwards, polarity changed when crossing the Equator and then increased again accordingly to the zones given on a map showing the Earth's magnetic field. In some parts of the world the zones were non-uniform, which I believed was caused by concentrations of Lodestone deposits.

All the changes were my responsibility and at times inconvenient. I forget the maximum power needed in the northern hemisphere but the machine on the DG was fully loaded producing more power than was generated on another dynamo for the ship's total electrical requirement. Thank goodness we had a third stand-by machine!

The system functioned quite satisfactorily but I became apprehensive when I noticed cracks appearing in the bitumen encasing the cables on deck, something to be expected after passing through the tropics and the constant flexing of the ship's plating. My qualifications as an electrical engineer didn't help my peace of mind being fully aware of the possibility of salt-water ingress and at 110V, most insulation in those days would have been susceptible to failure.

Our voyage at 11–12 knots, to Australia calling at Cape Town, Port Elizabeth, East London and Durban carrying war supplies and then on to Australia for food for Britain, progressed with the DG in use as required.

It was during the last leg, homeward bound, that I received ominous reports of smoke/steam was coming from the DG cables for'd. The inevitable had happened; I saw sparks and shorting at two of the cracks in the bitumen, so the DG had to be switched off for the remainder of the voyage! Our worries on that score, at the time, were shelved because the convoy was attacked on the fourth night out from Freetown.

It was May 1942 when we left Freetown, Sierra Leone in a six-knot convoy of 20 or 30 ships. The *Royal Star* was one of the larger ships (12 knots maximum) and our skipper, Captain T S Brown, was vice-commodore of the convoy. The two Naval escorts were a large ocean-going tug and an ex-Yankee weather patrol vessel capable of 16 knots.

The first three days were peaceful because the good old Sunderlands of the RAF from Bathurst patrolled the area around and ahead of the convoy each day departing in the evening with an Aldis signal of farewell and good luck. After the third day we knew we were on our own, out of the range of the RAF Albatross.

As third engineer I was in charge of the twelve to four watch affectionately called the Graveyard Watch. The fun and games started the next night because we could hear underwater detonations taking place, depth-charges or torpedoes sounded in the engine room like someone hitting the ship's side with a sledgehammer. I informed the bridge that the 'Black Cross Blacksmith' was about! (Often in windy weather we in the engine room could hear underwater explosions before the bridge.)

We found later that two ships had been torpedoed, one a tanker ablaze – not a pretty sight. In the morning a message from our senior escort (ex patrol vessel) was received, stating it was in difficulties. During the night's action a depth-charge had exploded prematurely near its stern, damaging the main reciprocating steam engine. Many of the holding-down bolts had sheared, which meant it could only operate at a reduced speed, and continued use would cause total failure.

Our skipper was asked to take the escort in tow so that emergency repairs could be carried out. A simple sounding request but as it proved during the morning, required a lot of skill and ship handling experience to execute. There was a moderate sea running but the weather was fine and the convoy continued at six knots. After some repositioning of nearby ships the Navy ship lined up astern of the *Royal Star*. The difficulties of establishing a tow were soon apparent and could be described more informatively by a deck officer. I was much impressed and proud of our two deck apprentices who transcribed instructions between the ships by semaphore. At first the Navy signallers were impatient with our lads' slowness and doubtful interpretation, a lot of flag waving – not understood! But our boys soon got into the rhythm and after the first half hour and long before the tow was finally established were showing the RN that they weren't as good as they thought they were!

We in the engine room were more interested in how the tow would affect the performance of the twin triple expansion reciprocating steam engines and guessed that the escort was in the 800 ton category. It was while we were discussing and watching the tow being secured that our chief Mr W Innes informed the general assembly that 'the watch keeping engineers should not blame inefficient combustion in the stokehold onto the towing job!' When I relieved the fourth, Mr Watkins, I mentioned the chief's remarks, to which he said: 'I wouldn't put it past the old blighter to send His Majesty's Royal Navy a bill for the tow with intonations of salvage charges pending!' It was not possible to make an accurate assessment of the extra power required but it was necessary to make an increase of two revolutions to the average 30 to maintain our position in the convoy.

Our interest in towing power dramatically waned when after midday it was known that a U-boat was surfaced ahead of the convoy and maintaining a leading position! Presumably she was one of the 24-knot class and any attempt by our remaining trawler to close was fruitless.

So there we were, a German submarine leading a British convoy with its senior escort vessel in tow, and the U-boat commander using its radio, calling up his pals to join him at his 'tea party'. At least I had an afternoon watch thinking that no violent disruption should occur in the engine room from one U-boat, but what about tonight? Our tow was released during the early evening with, we hoped, a benefit from its 'make-do-and-mend' repairs. It began to get dark about 9.00 pm and I presumed when our unwanted guest could not see, our commodore altered the convoy's course by signal on the ship's whistle, a pre-arranged procedure.

I had turned in, complete with life-jacket (there was no danger jumping from a height into the sea wearing the new kapok jacket, whereas the old cork block type could break one's neck) when about 9.30 pm, gunfire indicated some sort of trouble was afoot. I opened my cabin door and saw tracer bullets hitting the bow of our ship, fired by ships on our aft port quarter and following the general direction saw a submarine crash diving at a convergent angle to our course! I quickly hopped back into my cabin because the direction of the bullets was beginning to move aft. along the *Royal*'s side. The submarine was so close to our bow that I sat in the darkness of my cabin hoping I would feel the ship shudder as she hit it. No such luck!

Crash dive!

The U-boat captain had obviously aligned his submarine at right angles to the convoy's course, the ploy being to manoeuvre it between the rows of ships so that both fore and aft torpedoes could be used as the ships came towards him and into his sights. Even on the surface in this position the convoy's larger guns could not be brought to bear and any shooting could be more dangerous to the merchant ships than the submarine. When I relieved the fourth he told me he had received a double ring - full ahead - and had given both engines full throttle. Obviously to no avail. I spent a very uncomfortable watch knowing that at least one submarine was scouting around beneath our ships. I now know how a rabbit feels when a stoat is circling for the kill! I didn't hang about handing over to the second at 4.00 am.

There was more action during the early morning by our two escorts who had been in contact with a submarine and were hopeful of some success but with no positive evidence. Anyway, we had no further trouble. We just kept those beautiful sweet smelling reciprocating engines turning, their gleaming connecting rods, eccentrics, and cranks flashing until the convoy reached Liverpool.

Our safe arrival, with the DG inoperative, in the Liverpool Docks, 27 May 1942, with much needed food was ensured by the unsung heroes of the flotillas of RN minesweepers (Royal Naval Patrol Service); whose dangerous, monotonous, routine sweeping of the estuaries and shipping channels into the ports in all weathers must have saved the sinking of many ships. An energised device was trawled well astern exploding magnetic mines harmlessly, which were most effective in shallow waters, laid by the Germans during the night.

In retrospect, how vital that order was to alter the convoy's course to starboard for the safety of many seamen, ships and desperately needed supplies. Indeed as the *Royal Star* was in the first line of ships and a prime target it could have been curtains for me, even though I may not have been on watch at the time. My cabin and those of other engineer officers were positioned over the engine room, the target area for torpedoes.

So our grateful thanks to the Royal Navy's small ships who tried and did save the convoy, with many lives of merchant men and their ships. Our RN escorts were few, their small converted vessels slow, but the spirit, courage and determination of their crews' magnificence - they saved the convoy.

The *Royal*'s tow made its small contribution to the success story because it was, I believe, the senior escort that pressed home the attack that most likely damaged or sank the U-boat that led the convoy.

The *Royal Star* was aptly named one of the 'Old Battle Squadron'.

ss Royal Star

It would be interesting to know whether the two apprentices survived the War and progressed to command their own ships? Jenkins was a rugged cheeky type with plenty of spirit, but I can't remember the other boy's name.

Our chief engineer, Mr James William Innes, was awarded the OBE in June 1943 for long and meritorious service in the Merchant Navy and was commended when his ship, the *Royal Star* was torpedoed and sunk off Cape Bengut when in a seven-and-a-half-knot convoy from Algiers to Malta, 20 April 1944. Ironically, it was hit in the starboard side by aerial torpedo in the engine room and stokehold, one man being killed. Was he my old shipmate? Because Mr Watkins, a third engineer is in the list of 645 personnel, with an additional 78 gunners and 272 passengers lost at sea through enemy action in the book *Blue Star, 1939-1945* by Taffrail given to me when I left the company.

Chapter Nine

A Chapter of Incidents

WHEN I left the *Royal Star* to go on leave, I was asked to stand-by a new ship the *Empire Might*. I joined her July 1942, in the fitting-out basin of J G Kincaid & Co, Greenock, Scotland. She had twin-screw triple expansion engines with Bauer Wach exhaust turbines (to a Clan Line specification) and, presumably to reduce the import of fuel oil, was coal and oil fired, which proved to be a most difficult and dangerous arrangement to operate.

ss Empire Might

I reported to Mr Marsh/Marshall? who was the Chief Engineer standing-by the new ship, on a dismal June day 1942, whose first concern was to know whether I had arranged any accommodation for my expected stay of some weeks. Initial enquiries through the dockyard management proved negative and they explained that due to wartime conditions there was a floating population of many thousands in addition to the residents of Glasgow and the surrounding districts. Indeed, many service men were sleeping in very cramped quarters and it was commonplace for a number to share one bed, in fact it was not unusual for five to be in a double bed, three at the top and two at the bottom!

It was decided to try the chief's landlady for accommodation, a game-keeper's wife who lived in an estate house at Inverkip some miles down-river from Greenock. Gratefully I learned that she would gladly give me a room, but for the first night I would have to share my chief's bed until a separate room were prepared! For both of us it was Hobson's choice and an unusual experience. Some time before we took the ship on trials he was transferred to another vessel and I believe was later lost at sea through enemy action.

As third engineer, I was again responsible for all electrical equipment and after the *Royal Star*'s problems with the degaussing gear, my immediate interest, among many other things, was the DG installation. What a relief it was to find in comparison it was a Rolls-Royce system. The main horizontal and the two vertical coils had been installed within the hull in the shelter deck, the vertical on the aft, and for'd bulkheads of the engine room respectively, suitably enclosed in steel casing protected from damage and adverse weather conditions. Low voltage energy was provided by a direct current (DC) rotary converter; 110V–12V and the flux density and polarity changed by a simple control box near the set (duplicate on the bridge). Small coils fitted in the binnacle, shunted from the main system, neutralised any effect the DG had on the magnetic compass. The low voltage system provided magnetic fields requiring much reduced power and minimalised failure through insulation break-down. All adjustments were made by the bridge officer with occasional checks by me when the converter set was inspected.

On the maiden voyage it proved to be reliable and trouble-free for which I was very grateful because the more sophisticated machinery in the engine room and with three boilers on oil and three on coal, it was very demanding. Outward bound, unescorted and maintaining a speed of 15–16 knots was no picnic; in the stokehold trying to get the three firemen to slave on the coal boilers while one of their mates was sitting about watching the oil do all the work on his boilers.

The weeks standing-by the *Empire Might* enabled me to experience a little of the shore-side life in Glasgow and its environs. Many days of rain made me realise why the natives regularly wore stout weather-proof raincoats, double skinned on the shoulders and hats similar to Sou'westers. In the pubs, to see the customary pint and a dram drunk by the men in a ritual of tossing back the whisky in one gulp and shaking the last drops of spirit into the beer before drinking the first long draught. There was also a huge population of starlings who returned before dark each evening and roosted on the many ledges in large buildings in the city centre, resulting in droppings forming a slurry on the pavements, making walking very precarious underfoot and overhead.

Sea trials were successfully completed and the ship performed well, reaching her specified 16–17 knots on the measured mile, but some adjustment was required to the 'bottom-ends' on both main engines, mine and Mr Fraser the fourth engineer's responsibility on the following Monday morning. On Saturday the fourth had met a young lady at a dance and was invited to her home where he received the hospitality of her family. It was suggested that he would be welcome to return on Sunday for tea which was extended to a colleague to act as a companion for her sister. So I found myself on a blind date where arrangements had been made to meet the two girls on Sunday afternoon at a Blood Transfusion Service Centre.

Apparently one of the girls had volunteered to give a blood sample with a view to becoming a blood donor, hence the service centre venue. After being introduced to my blind date the fourth and I joined the long queue outside. The four of us chatted happily as we moved slowly forwards with the many volunteers and eventually, when inside, found ourselves near the desk where one's personal particulars were being taken. It was then that the three accompanying the one volunteer found it would have been embarrassing to excuse ourselves from the queue, especially as the fourth and I were in uniform. With some bravado we agreed to also give a sample, it would be no problem.

However, when I presented myself to give the thimble full of blood, the nurse explained that because of the wonderful response by would-be donors, to save time and expense, they had decided to take a pint there and then! To cap it all, a number of 'man-draulic' equipped trestle beds had been provided in addition to the two electrically operated extracting machines in order to reduce queueing time. I found myself on one of the former which, after the first half pint, free-flowing delivery, I had to produce the remainder with a clenched fisted right arm acting as a pump! Afterwards I was conducted to the compulsory ten-minute rest couch and given a weak cup of tea and biscuit.

Eventually we all joined up a happy group comparing our new experiences, but I found that some of the spring had gone out of my step! The tea and hospitality shown to us by the girls and their parents was first class and we all enjoyed the evening very much. On the long journey back to the ship by bus and tram, in the blackout we both felt very tired and agreed that the initial sparkle on meeting the girls had diminished somewhat after the 'blood-letting' ceremony and were grateful to reach our bunks onboard ship.

Monday morning 'turn to' was accomplished lethargically and the bottom-end bearing adjustment commenced on both main engines. This work always demanded a large physical input supervising the 'heavy gang' working with 15-pound sledges and a swinging 25-pound 'tup'; the fourth and I taking 'leads' and scraping the white metal bearings where necessary. After breakfast we both felt the effect of Sunday's donations; indeed Mr Fraser remarked that the term 'sweating blood' had lost its meaning in our case! Later, when our chief Mr R W Brown learned of our exploits, he remarked 'Any more blood-letting should be carried out after any demanding work was required on his beloved engines and large 'kettles' in the stokehold'.

A maiden voyage usually presents extra problems with new machinery's teething troubles and although great attention had been paid to clearing out remnants of the building process; rags, bolts and nuts, asbestos lagging, rivets and welding rod stubs, we soon had problems with blockage of the bilge suctions, during the first days at sea. The movement of the ship dislodged unseen debris from all levels in engine and boiler rooms, requiring many extra hours work removing it from tank top and bilges - difficult and dirty work.

I think it was the third day out when the starb'd wet and dry air pump developed a serious steam gland leakage reducing its function. A request was made to stop the starb'd main engine in order to repack the leaking gland - a difficult decision because we were in rough seas, unescorted and in potentially dangerous waters from submarine attack. Captain Phillips agreed with Mr Brown that the engine could be stopped next day with the port engine on maximum power, estimated to give a speed of 12-13 knots. All preparations were made and the repair carried out by us in an atmosphere of tension taking about 20 minutes, and with a sigh of relief all round when the starb'd engine's shiny cranks started flashing again at speed with the exhaust turbine engaging with a whine bringing the unit up to full power.

Our voyage to Australia, New Zealand via South Africa continued, but the management and operation in the stokehold was extremely difficult. One Scotch boiler developed tube leakage on a large scale and was taken off line and many leaking tubes re-expanded while still under pressure, an extremely hot and difficult job for the relays of engineers who could only work for short spells in the back combustion chamber. Unfortunately the boiler continued to give leakage problems in new areas. Finally Mr Brown decided to try an old remedy by emptying the boiler of treated water, refilling with sea water then steaming for at least 24 hours. Afterwards it was blown-down and returned to service with treated fresh water, which proved successful because resultant deposits from the salt water had sealed the tube expansions and the boiler gave no further trouble.

In my previous ships: *Stuart*, *Avelona* and *Royal Star*, cleanliness in and around the boiler fronts was meticulously maintained to ensure that no fire hazard occurred in the stokehold. The tanktops underneath the boiler fronts were painted white and illuminated - engineers on an incoming watch would not take over if a trace of bunker oil leakage was seen anywhere in the stokehold.

Every effort was made to keep some standard of cleanliness in the *Empire Might*'s stokehold, particularly in the oil-fired end aft. But this proved very difficult as all the boilers were in a common boiler room; ash and coal dust constantly pervaded the oil fired boilers. At Cape Town and later Durban, the bunkers were replenished with South African coal. It was my first experience with this fuel which had a 30%-40% ash content compared with the average 12%-15% of British coals. Ash boxes had to be emptied many times during a watch and the whole boiler-room was covered with a fine light grey dust, including personnel after an ash dumping session. Keeping the stokehold in a reasonable state of cleanliness under these conditions was an impossible task, so the possibility of unseen fuel oil percolating on to a tanktop or in a bilge with coal dust, was increased - a serious fire hazard.

At our last port of call before the long haul across the Indian Ocean: Beira, Mozambique, Portuguese East Africa, there were two German merchantmen at anchor across the bay from where we docked. I believe they had been there since the outbreak of War. The German ensign flown at their sterns looked peculiar and a scrutiny with binoculars proved them to be rectangular painted boards. Presumably the skippers had run out of replacement flags and produced the 'fixed' flags to advertise their presence to the British and Allied ships calling there.

We reached Melbourne after a difficult voyage; trying to maintain service speed but getting full steaming capacity from the coal boilers was difficult. Problems with the firemen rotating their duties so that they all took turns on the coal boilers proved to be fraught with human idiosyncrasies - a large percentage became 'sea lawyers' overnight!

After Melbourne a call was made at Sydney and then on to 'windy' Wellington, New Zealand. It was there while in harbour, that a minor earthquake occurred; it was my first and only experience (mildly frightening). It happened while I was down below in the engine room when the ship started to surge against the quay I rushed up on deck and for seconds watched buildings trembling, accompanied by an eerie rattling of roofing tiles, etc. It was an uncanny feeling to witness objects moving which before had always been as firm as houses!

While anchored awaiting a berth at Littleton, Christchurch, our final loading port, one of my colleagues was line fishing; he asked me to take over while he made a call to the 'heads'. He instructed me on how to sense by 'feel' on the line if it became 'engaged' and to make another cast when it drifted too far with the current. Retrieving the line for a cast, I enthusiastically swung it round like a bolas allowing the weighted line to slip through my fingers. It suddenly stopped in flight by a hook impaling in my finger! Being a non-fishing type, I did not realise that there were more above the two hooks near the weight. The heavy gauge hook had buried itself in my finger with the barb out of sight. I was detached from the line by Mr Davidson, the second engineer and, complete with hook and the second mate who was O/C first aid, went to the small hospital accommodation.

My case was examined carefully and the second mate was preparing lance, etc, to cut out the hook when fortunately for me, Mr Davidson thought the hook could be removed by cutting off the eye and then pushing the remainder through my finger, estimating it would miss the bone on the way through and save stitching. It was decided that this option should be tried first, pushing the hook through making a circular tour round the bone; the second returned with a pair of pliers with cutting facility and we all took a tot of local 'anaesthetic', an amber coloured liquid from bonny Scotland!

I was then seated in a chair with Mr Davidson sitting on me with my arm through his legs, the idea being that it would keep me firmly in place and unable to see the operation. The eye of the hook was cut off and I was allowed to see the first stage of my operation and a second tot of medicinal comfort downed. We then resumed our operating positions with the second mate holding my finger firmly on a table. The pushing then started and after two movements I was informed the barb was in sight; seconds later the hook pulled out so neatly that its entry and exit had to be pointed out to me and it was difficult getting iodine in to the holes. A celebratory tot of medicinal comfort was taken all round on a very successful operation with a sigh of relief from me and the second mate because he had not been keen to use the scalpel anyway. Thereafter my fishing colleague referred to me as 'The big one that didn't get away!'

We left Littleton fully loaded for the Panama Canal where the ship's passage was monitored by American Navy personnel, fully armed, in engine room and on the bridge with their own independent telephones and at liberty to shoot if a false manoeuvre were made - a sensible wartime precaution because any ship in the locks putting the main engines astern or ahead could seriously damage the gates. Once a merchant ship got under way the electric towing 'mules' would be unable to stop a few thousand tons hitting the gates, thereby putting a vital link between the Pacific and Atlantic oceans out of action; so important for the American navy and allied merchant ships to maintain a full scale war effort.

Our next rendezvous was New York for coal and oil and then forming a nine-knot convoy and finally joining another from Halifax when Captain Phillips was appointed assistant commodore. It was January and the North Atlantic provided its normal weather: fog, gales, sleet and snow in various combinations to suit anyone's taste! On a stormy night, in the early part of the voyage the *Might* was hit with a gigantic wave on the 4–8 watch. I was awakened with the emergency engine room bells ringing and, with other engineers slid down the ladders, found the second, on the dimly-lit operating platform in between the main engines, shivering, soaked to the skin with icy sea water. Apparently the heavy sea had flooded the boat deck, sprung the engine room skylights, sending a torrent of water down below, fusing lights on the way. Similar conditions had occurred in the stokehold. With torches we quickly established that no serious damage had been done, I took over the watch, when the second and men similarly soaked, went topside, to change into dry gear.

My immediate priority was to restore lights on some of the boiler water gauge glasses, not an easy task requiring the use of both hands which meant entwining one's legs in gratings to work in difficult positions on hot components with the ship lurching in all directions. In the meantime the fourth was in charge on the main engine platform monitoring engine revolutions, often checked every five or ten minutes and adjusted accordingly. Keeping station was always a challenge which entailed close co-operation between bridge and engine room, the engineer striving to keep an average engine speed, thereby reducing the need for speed changes from the bridge. In reasonable weather it became competitive between watches to record the least number of revolution changes.

On the second's return he related how frightening it had been, thinking the ship had been torpedoed, all hands thought their number was up! When he realised the cascade of water had stopped he rang the bridge saying to the mate, 'Are we in trouble?' who replied, 'No, but I think some poor blighter is from enemy action, on the starb'd wing of the convoy'.

To which Mr Davidson replied 'And we shall be if we take another one like that because we'll have no lights!' Anyway, the mate reassured him that rarely is there a repeat of rogue waves but would take action to minimise its effect if he saw another coming.

I then set about replacing fuses and burst light bulbs in the engine room; afterwards returning to wedge myself into my bunk.

In daylight we found we were the only ship with the commodore vessel, the storm had made it impossible for many ships to keep in position. The *Empire Might* had proved her ability to keep station in atrocious weather with the skill and seamanship of the bridge staff, contributed to by the engineers maintaining a constant engine speed, which was no doubt helped by the exhaust turbines preventing excessive racing. While we had had a very rough passage, we silently saluted the crews in the small vessels, destroyers, corvettes, and similar size merchantmen on being able to keep afloat, which they did and in dribs and drabs returned to their positions in the 6–9 knot convoy.

The rough weather continued with sea water temperature falling so much so that a layer of ice started to form on the inlet cooling water pipes, in the engine room, indicating to us that our course was way northwards and the bridge confirmed that Iceland was in the offing. I had never previously seen ice on pipes which had formed from the humid atmosphere in the engine room mainly contributed to by the gland steam from the exhaust turbines and illustrated that fresh water freezes before sea water.

We docked safely at Avonmouth on 6 February 1943 and with mixed feeling I left the ship to sit for my chief's ticket.

After the War I read with interest, from the book *Blue Star Line* by Taffrail, on her next voyage, that the *Empire Might* did suffer a stokehold fire. In May, in convoy off West Africa, fire in the stokehold caused loss of power and was given a temporary tow by a destroyer Under the direction of Mr Brown, the engine-room staff managed to get the ship underway at 12 knots, eventually reaching Dakar for repairs. I could visualise knowing the ship, how difficult and dangerous it must have been for the engine room crowd during their 12-day stint getting the *Empire Might* to Dakar.

Captain Phillips, chief officer Stratta and Mr Fraser were officially commended in the *London Gazette*, 19 November 1943 for their fine work. On 3 January 1945, Mr Brown was awarded the OBE for long and meritorious service in the Merchant Navy.

I returned to London to study and sit for my chief's ticket again staying at the British Sailors Society's hostel but because the LCC school of marine engineering, Poplar, had been damaged by enemy bombs, attended a school in Drury Lane. I believe it was an art/drama school because we made a striking contrast when entering or leaving the building with the young students on the third floor above ours.

Wartime conditions with all its restrictions, little food and entertainment, travel in the black-out, no doubt made it easier for me to concentrate on my studies in the evenings. However, I remember well an occasion when the monotony was relieved. Weekly dance evenings at our hostel always provided a pleasant time but some of the girls began to complain about a certain gentleman who was making improper advances and was not put off by their many rebukes. 'Ginger' and his pal, both I think, studying for their mates' ticket, decided to take action on behalf of the girls on the 'Mediterranean type' gentleman if he continued his advances the following week. He did, and a short sharp encounter ensued, when he was taken in hand, frog-marched from the building and dumped bodily into the horse drinking trough (still in use) on the traffic island in the middle of the road junctions. Both returning with the remark that they thought it would cool off his ardour, and it did.

Chapter Ten

THE FORGOTTEN SQUADRON

AFTER successfully obtaining my chief's ticket I was appointed second engineer of the *Norman Star*. She had been undergoing a major refit on the Tyne. Unfortunately I twisted a knee badly in the stokehold and was sent home on sick leave. Some weeks later I was asked to become a member of a crew to pick up a new ship built in the United States of America.

The War had dramatically changed the pattern of voyages of all merchant ships and because of the losses incurred by Blue Star Line and other companies, complete crews, officers and men, were sent to the USA to take over new ships built there.

Blue Star ships outward bound taking men, supplies and equipment to the ever changing War theatres were hair raising to say the least, but because they were refrigerated, after unloading were sent to collect food supplies, etc, which meant returning to the UK. This ensured a continued link with BSL management.

My war-time service, along with other BSL officers, took a unique turn when we became members of what we christened ourselves the 'Forgotten Squadron'. The *ss Samtay* was part of that squadron, on a bare-boat charter to the Ministry of War Transport. During the time I was on her (January 1944 until March 1947) we only returned twice to the UK, hence the term forgotten squadron. The last of our three voyages lasted one year eight months. It was the *Samtay*'s luck to get involved with another campaign in Indonesia long after the War hostilities ceased on 14 August 1945 - but that is another story.

The beginning of the forgotten-squadron era began for me when we disembarked from the *Queen Mary* during the third week in December 1943 and were accommodated in luxurious hotels. I was in one near Madison Square Gardens, the boxing arena. Murals in the public rooms depicted scenes from events in the pugilistic world, I think it is now called Madison Towers. The meals were lavish, many courses - breakfast included a plate of fresh oysters as a first course. Having seen the meagre diet the British people were existing on during my brief leaves, made me feel a bit guilty.

When entering or leaving the hotel a big contrast in temperature was experienced between plus 70°F and well below freezing point outside where some people, even though they were well covered, wore woollen ear muffs. Indeed it was too hot inside the bedroom for me, so after some difficulty a window was opened slightly, but during the early morning, quickly closed again! The bed clothes only catered for the high temperature.

My first priority was to purchase a safety razor because my two 'cut throats' along with other toiletry items had been stolen at Liverpool before we left. When we were told we were going to the States to bring back a new ship, a small suitcase had been packed with my requirements, as a passenger, for the outward voyage. The bulk of my clothes, uniform, etc, were in two larger cases. The small case had been stolen from the left luggage office at the Central Railway Station, Liverpool, but the police had caught a thief with a case. They picked me up at midnight and I was taken to see if it were mine. It was, but I was not allowed to take it as it was required as evidence for the court case that morning. Even though I explained that my train was leaving in an hour's time for an unknown destination, the best they would do was to make it the first case in the morning! So I had no option but to leave it and join the Special Forces' train to our secret destination. We had only been able to give our relatives a number for our future posting addresses.

Exploring New York was exciting but a little difficult because of our meagre finances. I think we were allowed 70 cents a day pin money, yet it cost two to six dollars for the cinemas but if in uniform, half price. At that time the exchange rate was $4 to the £1 Sterling and a hair cut cost $1 or 5/- (25p) when compared with (1/3d) just over 6p at home.

I was fortunate to spend Christmas and New Year with another engineer officer with his relatives at New Rochelle and Fall River, Massachusetts, whose hospitality was much appreciated.

Early in the New Year the splendour of the hotel and the excitement of this great city began to pall; boredom, having nothing to do and limited finances made me turn to looking for a job. As we had to be prepared to leave at a day's notice it restricted the choice of employment as it had to be on a day-to-day basis. Many officers took up relieving duties on American ships in port, others worked in the Red Cross, etc. In my case I thought it would be interesting to see what I could do on the open market and find out how an experienced marine engineer with a first class certificate of competency would fare outside his profession.

My apprenticeship had been in electrical engineering, so I first tried shops selling electrical goods but when the potential employer learnt I might want to leave at a day's notice – no luck.

After two days my ego was somewhat dented but I learned that other men had obtained casual labouring jobs at Sterns, the large department store. I was interviewed in Sterns' employment office and told to report next day at 8.30am and report to a Mr X, I would earn $4 a day, paid each day. Mr X turned out to be the manager of the ladies' shoe department on the first floor. I was sailing into uncharted waters! He introduced me to the two assistants who explained my duties were to remove shoes from their boxes – translate the size code in the shoe into the relevant number and width, eg 4A, 5B, etc. These I marked in the shoes, tied them together and put them into large cardboard boxes. Scores of brand new shoes had to be dealt with and made ready for a sale starting the following week. The ladies would then be let loose on all the boxes and they could buy two pairs for the price of one! Under no circumstances was I to attempt to serve, fit , or sell shoes to customers instructed the assistants, they emphasised that a shoe-salesman took years of training. Little did they know they were dealing with a Cordwainer's son!

My job was getting tiresome when I was approached by a young lady requesting service. I explained that I had only started that morning and was inexperienced. It could have been my English accent which aroused her curiosity, because she suggested as I had to learn sometime, why not now? I was launched! - and finished by selling the lady two pairs in an episode of pleasant exchange. The 'terrible two' had observed the closing stages of my maiden voyage with none too friendly glances. After my customer departed, I was instructed to concentrate on the decoding job and leave the sales strictly to them! I suppose I didn't help our relationship when I intimated that it was only the price of the shoes I required from them to complete my successful sale.

My shoes for sale continued to accumulate, but court shoes were difficult to fasten together so I asked a new assistant in the afternoon if they had a lace-hole punch available. He found one and was too busy to enquire what I wanted it for. I proceeded to punch holes in the court shoes in discreet positions and used them to tie the shoes together - after all they were cheap at half the price!

A flood of customers took place during the afternoon and as I was able to serve more ladies, I was beginning to enjoy my £1 a day job. But at one time an old lady (she must have been at least 45!), asked me where the service counter was (where purchases were wrapped). Not to show my inexperience now, I indicated to her a direction (I hadn't a clue where it was!). About ten minutes later a sharp loud voice was directed upwards to me: 'Young man, for your information the service counter is in that direction!' The smallish 'old' lady departed leaving me much reduced in rank, with a red face and wishing to hide behind the counter!

The next day I reported for work with happy anticipation but was told that the ladies' shoe department did not require my services! I wondered why, after only one day, I'd sold quite a few pairs of shoes to young ladies who seemed happy with their purchases, as well as my pre-sales task. I was sent to the top floor in the Notions Department, completely out of sight of all customers! My task in the Notions Department was to assemble customers' orders ready for despatch, which were received from all department sale counters. It supplied all sorts of gadgets, fittings, etc., mainly associated with the bathroom but also it included packages of ladies' toiletry requisites - my education continued to progress.

At the end of my first week at Sterns we received orders to move to Baltimore to take over a new ship which later turned out to be the *ss Samtay*, so it was back to more familiar duties - engines, boilers and North Atlantic convoys.

The Bethlehem-Fairfield shipyard had many slipways, something like 14 I think, and I was told that launching took place every other day. I was certainly impressed with the conveyor belt principle of mass production carried out on such a large scale. It was a huge assembly plant having acres and acres of space in addition to the slipways so that storage and preassembly of huge ships' sections could take place. It became quite clear how an average assembly time and launching of ships in a fortnight was possible. We discovered the *Samtay* had been assembled in 26 days, longer than the average, because of the encroachment of Christmas and the winter weather, well below freezing most days.

We boarded the *Samtay* during the afternoon and she was ready for sea trials the next day. Normally in Britain, senior engineers and deck officers stood by a new ship during the latter stages of its construction to familiarise themselves with the vessel's physical and technical intricacies.

This time takeover and sea trials were completed in 48 hours flat! I think, one of the most hectic, physical and mental two days I have ever experienced. We were suffered in the engine room as observers only and were not allowed to touch a thing. To make matters worse there were no senior engineers available who had a working knowledge of the complete engine room plant, asking questions was fruitless. The engineer in control of the main engine when asked for information said: 'Say bud, I just drive the godamnthing on trials!'

There were a number of minor plant malfunctions which were corrected American style, an example being a leaking boiler safety valve. Expecting it to be opened up and corrected for my approval the next morning, I found a new valve had been fitted and the boiler under steam! This principle was practical and efficient because of the standardisation of these ships.

We were told at Liverpool that we were going to the States to bring back a new ship - a short trip, so we thought. Our sailing orders at Baltimore soon changed that! We loaded at New York with stores and fighter planes on deck for the Mediterranean and made a second voyage to the same area, slow convoys all the way, before returning to the UK 11 months later.

Postcript

There is no doubt the Liberty ships made a large contribution to the War's outcome when some 2,700 were built and I understood about 200-300 British manned during the latter stages. Most had the prefix SAM in the ship's name, thought to relate to Uncle SAM (US) but I understand it was the British Ministry of Transport nomenclature - Superstructure Aft of Midships. A number of Liberty ships were adapted and used as tank carriers, aeroplane transporters, tankers and colliers by the US.

Assembly times averaged 14 days, the record was four days 15 hours. It was claimed after the War that the actual man hours building Liberty ships were similar to the British, constructing standard 'Ocean' ships in their cramped yards in conditions beset with black-out and air raids. With their 50- and 30-ton Jumbo's and large hatches they were real 'war horses' able to load, carry and discharge, tanks, all forms of transports and supplies independently.

After my first year on the *Samtay* when the main engine, boilers and most of the auxiliaries had been checked small assembly errors corrected (understandably because many were built in works with limited marine experience), she was a reliable and sound vessel. A weakness in the hull in line with the bridge perpendicular on the first dry docking, showed a slight deformation of the keel and double bottom strakes but from subsequent checks remained constant.

The *Samtay* served as a sea-going work-horse for 24 years and her Blue Star Line sister ship, the *ss Samnid* launched a week after the '*Tay*, was still sailing after 35 years and no report of her being broken up.

The American Liberty ship was built from a British design, originating from Sunderland where the first standard ships were built. (Ref. *Where Ships are Born*, Sunderland, 1346 - 1946 by J W Smith 'Blue Peter', and T S Holden. Printed by Thomas Reed & Co Ltd, Sunderland, Nautical & Engineering Publications.)

The Samtay *March 1947 at Curacao*

Chapter Eleven

GERMAN OCCUPIED CRETE

AFTER discharging our cargo at Alexandria, Egypt, on one of our voyages we were apprehensive upon learning our next trip was to Crete. It was general knowledge at the time that it was completely occupied by a large German force, a figure of over 10,000 men was quoted.

Our duty, however, was to take a small British force to Crete who were to take over the islands' administration. Although no official surrender had been obtained, an agreement had been made with the German force that they would take no offensive action, due it was rumoured, to them being cut off from receiving any further supplies, or support from their High Command, but they were fully armed and occupied most of the island. In return for the Germans taking a passive position the British High Command agreed to put a similar number of Allied troops on non-combatant service. Nevertheless, notwithstanding the rumours, for us the trip to Crete was not received with enthusiasm.

Included with the supplies, equipment and vehicles for the small British force were 300 tons of coal - an item which puzzled us. But our most valuable cargo was a group of Cretan women with several children. They were the wives and friends of the guerilla leaders who had continued the fight against the Germans while their women folk had been evacuated to Egypt.

There was no cabin accommodation for the women and children. It was decided that they should not suffer the confines of the ship's holds with the expeditionary force - so they were given the lower bridge wheelhouse. It wasn't very big for roughly 30 women and children, but returning to their menfolk after years of separation was worth any discomfort. In any event it was expected at the most, they would only have to tolerate the cramped quarters for two or three nights.

A certain tension of uncertainty pervaded the *Samtay* on our arrival at Crete and increased when we made an approach to Heraklion harbour.

In the engine room we were to be ready to give maximum full ahead power in the event of trouble, to make a hasty getaway from the island, the DEMS gunners at action stations. I was down below when entering the harbour, and from the engine movements knew that our skipper Captain Trevor Williams was going in stern first - a tricky manoeuvre into a small harbour with partly sunken vessels in awkward positions, with tension increasing as we became a more vulnerable target.

Thank goodness we had a good reliable triple expansion steam engine, which I knew from experience would give full power in seconds, changing from one rotation to the reverse by throwing over the reversing links with the main steam throttle valve full open. With this in mind the fourth was in charge of the boilers, the third on the reversing links and I on the main throttle. If an emergency full ahead were given (double ring on the

telegraph) the '*Tay* would leave the harbour with everything she'd got; she would certainly have moved the mud out of Heraklion harbour as good as any dredger, provided the DEMS gunners kept the steering gear flat in one piece from enemy attack!

We eventually tied up at the small quay but the watch below had to keep a full head of steam and ready to leave at a moment's notice. A full stand-by was maintained all the time during our few days in Crete.

The scene on the quay was something to be remembered, what a pity it could not have been photographed (no cameras or radios allowed during the War), the excitement of the throng of people, mainly Cretan guerillas, cannot be described. They looked a fierce lot in their black dress, pantaloon trousers, bandanna headgear, black unkempt full beards and armed to the teeth. Our DEMS guard on the gangway had difficulty stopping them from boarding until the official clearance was given. Seeing their womenfolk and children after those years of separation and hardship, and still alive, made their impatience understandable, some revolvers were fired into the air in celebration.

At last they were allowed on board, the reunions with joy and sadness were very touching. One character approached me with elation, took me up in a gorilla type hug, planting kisses on my cheeks, demonstrating his thanks in no uncertain terms, much to the amusement of my chief Mr Robert Reid (a large squarely built Scot), who was watching. I didn't mind the Ouzo-laden breath or the barbed-wire type beard scrubbing my fair skin, but the pressure of his live grenades (mills bombs) into my midriff and his bandolier of cartridges into my chest were painful to say the least. I was relieved in more ways than one when he put me down!

After all the joy and excitement of the reunion of these brave men with their families, the ship's routine returned to normal but stayed in a state of readiness to depart at a moment's notice. It was comforting to see a small

British Navy corvette accompanying us in the harbour, we must have been the first Allied merchant ship in Crete after hostilities ceased.

Shore leave was limited but I did manage to visit the airfield at the invitation of squadron leader Cox and his RAF officers whom we had entertained on-board previously. His total command was one Spitfire and an old Dakota, they were obviously the first RAF presence on the island, presumably to establish a line of communications between Crete and the Allied Command. Two of his officers were on special duties with language skills which enabled them to forage into the country and be in contact with the Germans.

There was a brisk business in buying any civilian clothing from our crew, particularly suits at attractive prices - we wondered who the recipients were.

Before we left, with some relief, there was a small official ceremony in the town to celebrate the arrival of the British force.

Postscript

In April 1973, my wife and I spent a fortnight's walking holiday in Crete with Heraklion and Chania as our bases. It was most enjoyable during April, not too hot and the spring flowers beautiful. Knossos, the remains of a Minoan city was particularly interesting.

Heraklion was recognisable and had not changed dramatically, but the harbour looked larger than when last I saw it. Language difficulties prevented me from establishing contact with anyone who might have remembered the *Samtay*'s visit, but one morning towards the end of our holiday, while looking around the harbour I found a customs officer who could speak a little English. He remembered the *Samtay*'s visit but he was only a small boy at the time, so there was no real exchange of information.

A vivid account of the guerilla's activities is given in the book *The Cretan Runner* by George Psychoundakis, translated by Patric Leigh-Fermor, published by John Murray.

Heraklion harbour 1973

Chapter Twelve

OPERA AT THE SAN CARLOS

THE huge shuttle service, of which we were part, carrying war supplies and personnel from Port Said and Alexandria, continued with the discharge ports becoming more Northern as the enemy was pressed back.

In April 1945 we entered Naples harbour which was littered with sunken vessels with every available buoy, and quay position taken up with ships discharging war supplies. Ships were moored stern on to the quays unloading into barges until space was available on some quays to unload tanks and heavy transport vehicles.

The retreating German and Italian armies were only a few miles North of Naples so a strict black-out and curfew was in force. Entry and exit to the docks was limited between 12.00 noon and 6.00pm for Merchant Navy personnel which caused some resentment but when ashore it was soon apparent the need for the restriction and only a few of the main thoroughfares were open to the forces and all side streets out of bounds.

Transport between ship and shore-side establishments was always difficult for us but the Army engineers who were responsible for loading and discharging the ships were most helpful and often invited us to join them when visits were made to the few places of entertainment available. Invariably we were invited to dine with them at their mess, a reciprocal gesture after being similarly entertained by us on board.

It came as a pleasant surprise when a visit to the opera was suggested. Special late passes were arranged and the chief and I found ourselves walking into the foyer of a world-famous opera house, San Carlos. It was my introduction to opera and I'm sure not in the best circumstances. Outside it was cold and wet and inside there were no carpets or heating, so the audience, totally service personnel, wore greatcoats and in some cases Balaclavas with caps on top, in order to keep warm.

Performing under such uncomfortable conditions must have required a valiant effort by the actors, singing in Italian to an audience, in the main like myself, who didn't understand the language or story of the opera. Added to the discomfiture no smoking was allowed, so at the interval the majority of the audience made an exit accompanied with much noise by the tramp of service boots on the bare boards. If and when one could get to a bar the only drink offered was a wine glass of a liquid which looked like water; thinking it was white wine the chief and I took a long draft and when we recovered, thought we must have removed some of the enamel from our teeth! We later discovered it was Streger, a liqueur, and accordingly cut down the intake rate but not to lose our place at the bar, ordered another glass. Strangely the second drink seemed to be smoother and after two more glasses we began to appreciate its warming qualities. Indeed on returning to the second act I thought I had acquired a glimmer of understanding of the opera *La Traviata* and whispered to the chief, that if he put an 'o' at the end of most of the Italian words they would be anglicised.

A later foray, with special passes, was to the Allied Officers' Club, Giardino Degli Aranci, Villanova, Napoli. There was a good mixture of forces personnel, mainly American and British with a sprinkling of females. A dance had been arranged and a short programme of entertainment by ENSA provided relaxation from war-time stress; my high spot was a dance with Cicely Courtneidge some years my senior, who proved to be a charming and sprightly lady.

Time passes quickly when one is enjoying oneself, and sometime after midnight we were offered a lift back to our ship by a British army captain who was accompanied by an American lieutenant. Needless to say he insisted we had a drink - one for the road - at his mess which we found was in a beautiful mansion with an internal courtyard. There we were introduced to some of his brother officers, a second lieutenant attending to our requests with the normal courtesy and deference to rank status. After an interesting interlude the American lieutenant in whose jeep we had been given a lift, suggested we must then have 'a drink for the quay' at his mess.

We were again impressed with the beautiful house the American officers had for their quarters but could not help noticing the contrast in protocol between these officers and the ones we had just left. Here they addressed one another using Christian names and the colonel attended to our drinks, while our lieutenant lolled against the bar.

Eventually we were driven to the dock gates during the early hours thanking our lieutenant and bade him good luck; there was a lot more fighting ahead for our forces. It was a long walk to our ship and when I got to my cabin and switched on the light I was shocked to see another fellow in my bunk. Within seconds seeing unfamiliar things in the cabin I realised I was on the wrong ship! With profuse apologies I made a hasty retreat just beating the chief to the gangway and after passing two more Liberty ships we found the *Samtay*.

Chapter Thirteen

WAY OUT EAST

I WAS still serving aboard the *Samtay* in the Mediterranean when the war in Europe ended in May 1945. We had all hoped to be returning to normal Blue Star Line peace-time duties when we arrived back in England later that same month, but the continuing conflict in the Far East prevented this.

So after only a few days leave we found ourselves sailing from Birkenhead in July with war supplies for the Asian theatre, travelling via the Suez Canal. Convoy procedure was adopted upon leaving the Red Sea and was continued until we reached Bombay. After unloading we found, with mixed feelings, that the *Samtay* was to be used to carry troops for the imminent invasion of the Dutch East Indies. Work was in progress fitting out the shelter decks to carry army personnel.

I think we had been in Bombay about a fortnight when, much to our relief, Japan surrendered on 14 August. So once again we looked forward to returning home after the long war years at sea, but it was not to be. Had we known at the time that it would be 19 long months before we saw our homes and families again I think we would have been even more depressed.

The decks were cleared of the bunks previously intended for the troops and the *Samtay* was loaded with food and army supplies for the Indies, sailing via Singapore. To ensure our well-being the entire crew were vaccinated against smallpox in one fell swoop. It was pointed out to the medical men that a staggered vaccination, conducted over two or three days, would ensure that any side effects would not all occur at the same time. Unfortunately our request was ignored and some days later the ill effects of the vaccination put the manning of the ship in some jeopardy - so much so that we had to put into Trincomalee for a couple of days to recover.

We called at Singapore and continued on to Surabaja, being among the first merchant ships to enter after the Japanese capitulation. The colourful sights and exotic smells of Java proved unforgettable and even now I can vividly recall how the 'go down' where we tied up was pervaded by an overpowering scent of cinnamon.

In the morning before breakfast it was always my custom to take in our new surrounding from the boat deck. Imagine my surprise, when looking down onto the quay, as far as the eye could see it was packed with hundreds of stark naked Japanese soldiers carrying out their ablutions at the water hydrants. This was our first sight of the former enemy face to face and it was literally minutes later that someone said 'Some of them are wearing hats'; a fact previously not noted until our gaze was directed to that area!

We noticed that Javanese women were walking quite nonchalantly through the throng of Japanese POW's as they conducted their early morning ritual; and after the first morning we also lost interest - a good example of how the unusual can become mundane within a short space of time.

Another highlight of that first visit was within a few days of our arrival, the atmosphere around and particularly within the ship's confinement became overpowering with cigar smoke. A British Navy guard had been placed on one of the sheds on the quay which stimulated the interest of our crew. Our first indication that a new enterprise had started was when I noticed practically all my men were smoking cigars instead of the normal cigarettes or 'Holy rollers'. But the image of them looking like successful businessmen was made a little incongruous by their chainbreaker vest and dungarees. The cigars were large and top quality, manufactured by Mondi Victor Company.

Apparently there were cases and cases of cigars of all grades and quality in the guarded shed, and obviously a 'special arrangement' had been agreed between the RN and MN. There did not appear to be a guard on the hundreds of Japanese prisoners but the cigars were an illustration that market forces applied!

It was the first and only time that I had seen individual mahogany boxes of cigars hermetically sealed within tin boxes. The cigars were kept in superb condition by this method, presumably necessary for tropical climates. I kept two boxes for months but they were officially bonded by the customs at South Shields when we finally arrived home. It was my intention to claim them when a weekly tobacco allowance was made, but I was sent on a long leave with instruction to stand by a new ship being built at Birkenhead. I often wondered who were the lucky smokers of my Mondi Victors!

There was limited shore leave while the British forces established its administration and soon found itself fully stretched coping with the Japanese surrender.

After unloading, it was back to Singapore where it became clear that the *Samtay* would become part of a regular supply service to Indonesia. Our voyages were short, two or three days with two or three weeks in port loading and discharging, which meant we had to cope with the tropical condition shoreside.

We soon found that the exotic plant vegetation we admired was accompanied by high humidity and an enormous insect population which invaded our quarters at every opportunity. No doubt an entomologist's Shangri-La, but for us a constant battle to keep the blighters at bay! Not only were there millions of them, but the few that we could recognise, such as cockroaches, looked ten times bigger than any we had seen previously.

One of the first things we learnt in this inhospitable climate was that painting activities on the ship had to be completed early in the day so that the paint was passed the tacky stage before nightfall. Even then insects might spoil the finish. For instance, a section of outside accommodation had been painted a brilliant white, but next morning it was completely black with a thick mass of trapped, mostly dead insects. The deck lights had attracted them.

Mosquitoes were a constant problem, so early each evening a regular 'insect action stations' was carried out. All cabin accommodation was fitted with mosquito doors and gauze wind chutes for portholes. With doors closed and accommodation vacated the cabins and alleyways were filled with a fog of insecticide. There were always a few 'Blenheim Bombers' (as we called them) which could only be knocked out by a concentrated attack with more than one Flit gun. The bodies of these insects were as big as one's little finger, with wings like a dragonfly's - and they certainly took a lot of killing.

Wickerwork furniture was very popular, particularly chairs as they were cool and comfortable. We acquired some from our Army Corps friends who were responsible for discharging and loading the STO cargo. The chairs had been in use for some time when we noticed that anyone sitting in one suffered more than the usual insect bites - with a concentration of bites occurring behind the knees when wearing shorts.

After careful observation it was found that there was a teeming population of bloodsucking blighters living in the chairs which were seen to retreat into the wickerwork jungle after making a meal of us! So we took turns at sitting on a chair as bait, leaping up at the first nibble so that a colleague could attack the precise spot with insecticide spray. We hoped that would be the end of our troubles and for a short time it seemed we had won. But either the chairs had become reinfested or the enemy immune to the insecticide, for we were soon once again unable to sit in them long before coming under painful attack.

There must have been some kind of solution because the Javanese used such furniture extensively. Anyway, our solution was to make a funeral pyre of the chairs on the quay!

On our second trip to Indonesia, Batavia, we were able to travel into town. There were a few shops open but there was practically nothing in them to buy. However, in the market place, displayed on the ground by native entrepreneurs, were all sorts of goods which apparently had been buried in the ground during the occupation. There were some items of female underwear and I bought a two-way stretch with diaphragm support for one of my aunts.

This interest in female apparel had been developed because of the shortage of such things during the War and pressure brought to bear on we innocent seafarers by our respective tribeswomen. A pair of silk stockings was a real luxury after having to colour their bare legs and getting someone to draw an imitation seam down the backs to give some dignity!

It was quite common for an unmarried officer to be delegated the task of purchasing lingerie for his married colleagues and was given a list of their wives' vital statistics. If on occasion resistance to undertake such duties occurred, rank was pulled on the unfortunate officer. It was explained to him that it was part of his apprenticeship!

Our frequent visits to Java with many days discharging and loading return cargos for Singapore, became very monotonous. Visits ashore were limited due I think, to the change-over from British to Dutch administration. There was no scope for sightseeing trips and because of the unstable political situation, no entertainment was available.

Singapore, however, was beginning to provide some civilian activities, shops, bars, etc. The Chinese Theatre was one attraction which provided me with a first-time experience of its unique presentation. It reminded me of my opera debut in Naples but the odd drink did not improve my interpretation or its entertainment value. At least the continuous performance 'open all hours' meant that one could join the audience knowing no objections would be raised, reminding me of my teenage days at the cinema. But I'm afraid, with the strident music giving me no pleasure and the constant scene shifting while the actors were on stage, was no help to make 'head or tail' of what was going on! I wonder whether scene shifting between acts and sometimes during the performance, that our present-day theatre was copied from the Chinese practice?

I think it was Singapore where I was introduced to 'Sew-Sew' girls, most of them charming and industrious old Chinese ladies sometimes accompanied by their daughters, who provided an onboard clothes repair service. A combined laundry facility was also available if required. The ladies would find suitable corners sitting cross-legged plying needles and thread vigorously giving an immediate cheap service. Positions near the galley were popular, perhaps the cook and his staff were able to get a discount! This unusual service was an example of how the Chinese in many parts of the world seem to find a niche for a cheap and reliable service; even Burslem, in my childhood had a Chinese laundry. I well remember the green covered window with its Chinese name where every week I took my father's stiff-collars to be laundered and watching two Chinese characters painted on a slip of coloured paper and given one half as my receipt. I believe most towns in England had a Chinese laundry similar to today's Chinese restaurants.

Chapter Fourteen

SAMTAY GOES ORIENTAL

華人的山地號

OUR activities around the Indian Ocean continued moving supplies to Singapore and Indonesia. However, as time passed our original crew became depleted through illness, both deck and engine room were affected. Replacements appeared to be impossible and on some trips I had to train DEMS gunners to act as firemen. Eventually it was decided that the remaining British crew be sent home - were they pleased - and replaced with Chinese. My petty officer storekeeper/donkeyman volunteered to stay.

CHINESE CREW 華人船員

The new crew were signed on in Singapore. Unfortunately there were only two Chinese stewards with some knowledge of English and I had one man with a limited understanding of our language. None of us understood Han or Cantonese, what's more, as I discovered later, the two languages caused misunderstanding between crew members. This was apparent when I asked one of the stewards to prepare a list in Chinese of the engine room cleaning duties for each watch. When I put the notice on the engine room noticeboard, puzzled frowns appeared on some of the men's faces. Ho Lung, my greaser, grinned when he saw my signature over the caption 'Second Engineer' and indicated by gesticulation that to him I was 'two motor cars'.

The Chinese calligraphy had reversed our order of rank. Mr Plant the young fifth engineer, was strutting about with a smile saying 'me five motor cars, the chief only one'. But it disappeared when I suggested 'one tank Mr Plant and he'll expect an increase in your output with all that extra power you've acquired!'

We couldn't blame all the problems on interpretation onto our new crew which was illustrated many times later. One incident when a small fuel oil leak occurred, I sent Ming Ti for some sawdust to soak up the oil and clear away the residue. He returned unable to find it but was sent back accompanied with the storekeeper, both returning with the sawdust. Ming Ti showed his annoyance because of his 'English puzzle' indicating that it was not sawdust but wood dust! Those early days of breaking-in our crew were very demanding and required tolerance, something which proved useful in later years. Trying to understand another country's culture and customs was educating and I am sure helped to modify one's views and perhaps improved one's tolerance on many subjects related to a foreign country. Thank goodness our ability to gesticulate our instructions and in the engine room to sketch on the noticeboard some of the mechanical plant functions, enabled the men to understand and successfully carry out their duties.

At sea the chief and I would have tea and biscuits at three bells (9.30pm) before turning in. It was arranged for the 8–12 fireman, when he came 'topside' for the watch's requirements, to also make the chief's tea. Hung Lo Won was instructed and carried out this ritual. In port when sea-going watches were suspended, I made it.

The first three-day trip from Singapore to Batavia was completed and sea-going watches changed to day work. Both the chief and I were taken by surprise when Hung Lo Won arrived at three bells, breathing heavily, and completed the tea-making operation. He was, of course, off duty and had apparently rushed back to the ship to complete his watchkeeping duty! I had difficulty explaining to him that the tea-making was only his duty when on sea watches. It had been difficult establishing the watch routine, breaking it had also to be checked.

A clean engine room and stokehold decreases the risk of fire and makes mobility within the confined spaces safer. For some time it had become difficult obtaining cleaning rags, cotton waste, etc, and during one spell petered out altogether. This situation proved to be no problem for Ho Lung, my greaser. During one watch he appeared with a discarded sack from the galley and cut it up into small squares. Then during the watch, between his oiling duties, squatted on his haunches and laboriously teased the strands apart making hessian waste, quite suitable for his cleaning requirements.

Eventually our Chinese crew settled down and both the mate and I found they carried out their duties very satisfactorily, they were totally reliable, particularly in port.

A SUICIDE 自殺

However, we did have a distressing incident in Padang, Sumatra, a few months later, one of the deck crew committed suicide. There had been some disturbance among the crew which did not interfere with the ship's operation, but because of the language difficulties we were unable to establish the cause.

During the late morning there was a commotion at No 4 hatch and the Indonesian stevedores came pouring out on deck greatly agitated. On investigation it was found that as they removed the cargo from the shelter deck a body was found hanging in the ladder hatchway. Mr Gee the first officer had the very unpleasant duty of removing the body for, regardless of his commands none of the crew would help in any way. The implication behind this attitude strengthened our worry that the reasons were well known by some crew members why the poor man took his life. Mr Wright the second mate helped him to remove the semi-naked body from the ladder hatch, a very difficult and unpleasant task in the hot humid atmosphere. It was put in the hospital in the poop deck.

At that time the political, military and civil situation was very unstable. The British had been progressively handing over to the Dutch colonists, whom the Indonesians were strongly resisting and, to make matters worse there were still Japanese in the surrounding hills who had not surrendered. Chinese were unwelcome ashore so no leave could be given to our crew. In these difficult circumstances the problem of disposing of the body had to be solved quickly since putrefaction sets in quickly in the tropical climate.

BURIAL AT SEA 海葬

Our skipper Mr Trevor Williams in agreement with the military authorities, decided that the only solution was a burial at sea. It was arranged that a tank landing craft would be used and the British Army (an Indian regiment) would provide a guard of honour on the barge which would sail a short distance outside the harbour for the burial ceremony.

Mr Gee was in charge of the burial. None of the crew would help to prepare the body for burial, but his Chinese bosun made a canvas bag. The day after the tragedy Mr Gee approached me to help so after a spot of 'medicinal comfort' to fortify us against the smell, etc, we went to the hospital. We were both stripped to the ~~waste~~ WAIST and while the mate held the body up I was guiding the lower part into the canvas bag when he accidentally dropped it, so he said! Quite a shock for me when it draped itself over my bare back! We eventually managed to complete our unpleasant task putting heavy Warwick screws inside the bag to ensure it sank. The skipper and chief joined the mate and myself for a few tots of 'medicinal comfort' to kill any unwanted germs after our pre-funeral duty.

When the funeral arrangements were made known to the crew they all wanted to attend, so as many as could be spared were given permission. Our Mr Gee who I'm sure had a little of Doyly Carte in his makeup, decided to put the text of the burial service inside a copy of the International Code of Signals, an impressive red-bound book, to impress the mourners, he explained, 'they wouldn't understand the English service'.

The following day the small landing barge came alongside and the body was put on board, draped in the Red Ensign. It departed seawards with Mr Gee in charge, the Indian guard of honour and mourners in the well of the vessel.

We later learned that the burial went off with less than the usual solemnity. The Indian soldiers were standing with Mr Gee on the raised sterndeck, overlooking the well of the vessel, with the mourners below. The body, on a board and draped in the Red Ensign, was held on the gunn'el at shoulder height by some of our crew.

Unfortunately for all concerned, the subaltern had not instructed the guard to fire the volleys of (live) ammunition simultaneously and heavenwards. So at the point when the salute was made the rifles were discharged at random to all points of the compass, over the heads of the mourners who dived down with the body among them.

Some understandable chaos ensued, but a second attempt was successful in committing the body to the deep. However, in the now nerve-wrought situation, somebody forgot to retrieve the ensign.

Poor Mr Gee was not complimented by the skipper when he returned because it was the only new Ensign we had left. Later we sympathised with him when he said 'I didn't think the old man would have bothered about the ruddy Ensign. With all that haphazard firing going on, I realised that anyone in the surrounding hills - Japs, Dutch or Indonesian, would have assumed that a naval landing was taking place, not a funeral!'

We departed Padang with the last of the care-taker British forces with their equipment for Singapore. Perhaps we would receive orders to return home?

Chapter Fifteen

SHEEP AND A SHEARING

WE had nearly finished loading on one of our trips to Indonesia when it was learned that a few hundred merino rams had to be taken from Singapore as deck cargo.

The War had not long ended and there were many Indian regiments occupying Sumatra and Java who for religious reasons would only eat mutton which had been killed under the supervision of their priests according to strict religious ritual. Because of this supplies of meat had to be transported live to the troops wherever their regiments were based.

Regular voyages were made by proper livestock-carrying ships from Australia to central points (in this case Singapore) for the sheep to be distributed by conventional cargo ships, to the various troop bases when only short trips were necessary. I believe this way of carrying livestock was stopped when arrangements were made for the slaughtering ceremony to be carried out in Australia. After this the meat was transported frozen, suitably identified for Indian army consumption.

It proved quite a sight when our consignment of Merinos arrived on the quay herded by many small boys and everyone was interested to see how the loading would be carried out. The ship's decks were many feet above the quay and there were no lifting cradles to be seen, but the boys soon showed that loading the rams was no problem.

A sloping gangway was placed between ship and quay, suitably side-roped, when one of the boys appeared with a sheep (presumably a ewe) on a lead. He then proceeded to circulate among the rams who immediately took an interest in his sheep and then walked up the gangway with a continuous stream of rams following. It was amazing how quickly this method worked in getting the large curly horned animals on board - as I remember, about an hour. Once started, the chain of sheep continued with an occasional break when the boy had to repeat his enticing process, apparently a few of the rams were blind and lost the stream at the gangway.

Our short voyage to Java was soon over with no problem with the sheep. They made a colourful sight, a carpet of deep red moving bodies and beautiful curved horns waving, the outer layers of their fleece impregnated with the red dust from Australia. They did not appear to suffer from the tropical sun - I wondered whether the thick wool layer insulated them from the hot atmosphere.

Preparations to unload the sheep were quickly made along similar arrangements used at Singapore. However, it soon became clear during the first half-hour that no form of pushing and shoving by the stevedores would get the rams to walk down the gangways. Calls for assistance from the deck officers were met with some enthusiasm from some of us, who were prepared to enter the seething mass of sheep. Thinking about it afterwards, what the scene must have presented to an onlooker was as good as any

Keystone Cops or Charlie Chaplin comedies! Here we were stripped to the waste trying to manhandle the sheep onto the gangways with their horns getting entangled with the ropes and up our shorts, quite a dangerous situation I can assure you! Even when a ram was physically frogmarched down a gangway no way would any of the others follow. What our chief officer would have given for that small boy from Singapore with his pet lamb on a lead!

The pantomime of manhandling the sheep with the assistance of the Indian Army continued throughout the morning with frequent breaks for the men to regain strength and replace liquid losses. We had given up after the first half-hour's foray, but as the number of sheep decreased on deck, this gave them greater scope to evade capture. So a certain officer started a betting school with a stop watch on how quickly a particular man took to capture and get a nominated ram onto the quay.

It was a steeplechase with a difference, winches, hatch-combings, etc., providing the jumps!

It was late afternoon before the last of the sheep departed. A good lesson in tricks of the trade was learnt that day at Surabja. One small boy with his sheep (having an essence of sex appeal), trotting about for an hour was equal to dozens of men struggling for at least five hours to do the same work!

There was no entertainment of any sort in Java while we were there and the only way of breaking the monotony were occasional visits to the Army officers' mess, where sometimes ladies were present, mostly service women. We in the *'Tay* would reciprocate by inviting some of them for dinner and drinks on board at a later date.

It was during one of these visits that our chief officer 'Jimmy the One', met his Waterloo. The Army officers had brought along with them a few Australian nurses who really appreciated the meal on board, it being a welcome change from the routine forces food.

Sometime after dinner the Chief Officer came into my cabin, which was next to his, with one of the nurses who had decided the removal of his beard would improve his appearance. This lovingly tended growth was his pride and joy, a full, black navy-style beard giving him a piratical appearance. Indeed it did make him look fierce and he always kept it neat and tidy and told me it had been cultivated and nurtured for at least six years. Knowing this, I persuaded the nurse, whom I could see had a sense of purpose about her, that he would surely regret his reckless act of bravado the next morning. So they rejoined the rest of the party.

Sometime later, they returned with a renewed request for a shearing to take place and I was to adjudicate and see that the safety of our Jimmy the One was taken care of during the operation! Apparently a bet had been made between them that the lady nurse from 'down under' would smoke and inhale, puff-for-puff, one Burmese black cheroot in tandem with the pirate chief.

Everyone in on the act expected her to be sick after the first puff, but to the amazement of everyone including the mate, she not only smoked it down to the last half inch, but asked for another one!

So our chief officer being a gentleman said the shearing must take place. I think secretly he was really curious to see what he would look like shorn; it never crossed my mind what the Aussie nurse would have forfeited had she lost the bet!

Before the shearing commenced the ceremony was launched with an all-round toast of double gin and tonics given by nurse 'Sweeny Todd'. It was obvious from the start that smoking Burmese cheroots was not her only skill; cutting and shaving hair from the body beautiful was another forté.

The removal of the prize beard was carried out with a flourish and provided quite some entertainment because it was taken in stages, depicting various characters; from the Count of Monte Christo, Dracula, Charles II, Farmer Giles, General Smuts, of course Hitler, Charlie Chaplin and I think finished with Olly Hardy. At each stage the patient was allowed a view of nurse Sweeny's handiwork and toasted with a round of drinks. To me as master of ceremonies it was becoming clear that the pirate chief was losing his fierceness as more hair was removed. Fortunately he was in a gay mood, but I was a little concerned when he would see himself sober, in the mirror, in the morning sunlight. In his full 'nakedness' he looked a babyfaced, young, inoffensive man with two double chins which gave him a benevolent look. At the end of our nurse Sweeney's operations she proposed a vote of thanks to her gallant patient with a final round of drinks and a request for another Burmese cheroot!

The next morning everybody from the skipper down, was really concerned with the mate's possible reaction when he saw himself in the mirror and, believe me, it wasn't good! The combination of the after effects of the party and his new babyface image proved very negative. He came into my cabin with a terrible look of repentance on his face and said 'My God I'm going to give it a coat of red lead and anti-fouling paint and regrow my beard as quickly as possible!'

Our Jimmy the One was never the same after the shearing even when he re-established his fierce image; to all of us especially to his deck hands the cutting edge of his authority had been blunted.

Merino ram

Chapter Sixteen

HIROSHIMA

AT the end of April 1946 we learned that the *Samtay* was required to take a small British Army contingent with its transport to Hiroshima. We received the news with a sense of curiosity, wondering just what scene would confront our eyes at the devastation where the first atom bomb had been dropped in anger.

Sailing from Singapore we reached the Japanese port of Kure and docked alongside the naval base which covered a large area. There were many workshops and we were informed that one of the measures to maintain security under the former militarist government had been to require the workforce and their families to reside in the area throughout their lifetime; in other words, people living in the Kure Peninsula were never allowed to travel outside its boundaries.

Sightseeing was limited within the precincts of the naval base but it was necessary to walk through some of the construction areas to reach public transport to Hiroshima. I remember vividly, as we walked through the shipyard, seeing about 20 midget submarines at various stages of construction. Although it was nine months since the end of the War, the sight of these sinister underwater killing machines revived the mental anxiety we had suffered being at the receiving end of torpedoes from similar boats. It was rumoured that the atomic bomb had been intended for Kure, but a slight breeze had caused it to drift over Hiroshima about 12 miles away.

My visit to Hiroshima, in the company of two fellow officers (seen in the photograph), lives on in my mind to this day. The picture clearly shows the total destruction suffered by the city, yet life somehow went on among the ruins and in the background can be seen a tram running along what appears to be the remains of a main road.

The only buildings standing were those of modern western-style construction - built with steel and concrete. Most Japanese buildings at that time were single storey and constructed from wood with tiled roofs, extremely vulnerable to the fire storm which followed the atom bomb attack.

When we entered the building from which the photograph was taken, on the wall at the side of the entrance doorway was a silhouette of a crouching figure. A person's body had shielded the concrete from the flash of the bomb leaving a permanent contrasting stain.

The visit was a short one, for the destruction and subsequent clearance of what remained, left nothing else of interest to see. There was an atmosphere of overwhelming desolation and I remember that we only walked a short way along the tram-track before boarding a tram to return to the bus terminus.

From left to right: Mr Waine third mate, Mr Tipping third engineer, SWS

Flame of peace
(Japan Information and Cultural Centre)

Hiroshima flower festival
(Japan Information and cultural Centre)

Our return journey to the ship was a quiet one, with little conversation. All three of us were weighed down by sombre thoughts of what we had seen and its implication for the future of the planet if any nation should ever use such a device again. However, the fact remains that the atom bomb helped to bring the war to an end, saving many lives - including, perhaps, my own. (I would have been involved in the aborted invasion of the Dutch East Indies.)

Hiroshima has since arisen from the ashes as a thriving metropolis in booming modern Japan, although the horror of 6 August 1945 will never be forgotten. Every year on that day a peace memorial ceremony is conducted when all citizens pause for a few moments of silent prayer.

Chapter Seventeen

French Leave - Chinese Style

BEFORE leaving Kure, Japan, we learnt that the *Samtay*'s duty carrying Army vehicles had been curtailed and that we would be making a call at Hong Kong for the sand ballast with temporary wooden floors on top to be removed from all five holds. This arrangement had been made to give stability when carrying, in the main, bulky military motor transport.

Our Chinese crew had been a little animated to hear that we would be going to Hong Kong since most of them, like ourselves, had not seen their families or been near their native soil for many months.

Kowloon wharves and godowns 1945. The hospital ship Oxfordshire *which carried POWs and internees back to the UK, can be seen in the foreground*
(Hong Kong Information Services photograph)

The large buildings, offices and warehouses attest to the richness of the old Far Eastern possession: few if any, were damaged during the war. From Kowloon, many British prisoners and internees were repatriated after liberation from Japanese camps. The *Oxfordshire* was equipped with the latest operating theatre and X-ray apparatus. She normally carried 505 patients and among her complement were eye, nose and throat specialists. Her displacement was 8,645 tons and a speed of 15 knots.

We tied up at Kowloon during the afternoon and the work of discharging the sand commenced.

Contrary to common belief by most Europeans that Chinese have inscrutable countenances is a misnomer their characteristics vary like all nations. The next morning, when I went down below, my storekeeper greeting me with animation, a concerned look on his face, asking 'Mr Swain, have you noticed any difference this morning?' It became apparent immediately to me that the men on duty were all complete strangers; we found that our original crew had vanished and had been replaced by a batch of 'stand-ins', even at breakfast we were served by stewards we had never seen before!

Naturally the mate and I were very annoyed for the change over had taken place without our knowledge and our authority had been ignored. When we attempted to find out what was going on we were met with a barrage of 'No savvy sir'. After lunch the situation was discussed with the skipper and my chief; the mate and I reporting that the work routine was progressing satisfactorily much to our surprise. Perhaps it was our stoicism, which we had developed from our crew which helped us to decide, to take no action and review the situation the next day. However, we were still worried about sailing day, estimated to be in a week's time, for we couldn't leave with an unsigned crew. We agreed that our departed crew were too astute to leave their accumulated earning to their 'stand-ins', the British Merchant Navy pay was very good by Chinese standards.

Amazingly, the ship's work routine, deck, engine room and catering, progressed just as smoothly as before with just the odd problem here and there which was solved by our customary pantomime of gesticulation. We strongly suspected the Hong Kong stand-ins knew a jolly sight more English than our departed crew, but the 'No savvy, sir' and 'come velly fine, sir' persisted.

Sailing day arrived and shortly after breakfast the *Samtay*'s crew literally changed on the quay! Here were our absentees paying off their stand-ins with just the odd disagreement and money changed hands in a remarkably smooth transaction.

The Chinese 'bush telegraph' had worked well, ensuring the punctual return of our men on a sailing date which had been indeterminate.

We had learned a further lesson on the Oriental way of doing things and couldn't help admiring the obvious trouble taken with instruction during the secret changeover to ensure everything worked well. I expect they knew that if they had asked permission for leave from us it would have been refused, especially if we had known how far some of them would be travelling to see their kinsfolk.

Some days after leaving Kowloon our stewards said they would like to provide a traditional Chinese meal for us as a gesture of appreciation for the crew's unofficial leave. We agreed it would have been churlish not to accept the proposition, but most of us were a bit apprehensive of the kind of dishes which may be put before us. These misgivings were based on a first-hand knowledge of the very unusual items we had found in the crew's quarters during the routine weekly cabin inspections. There were some very peculiar pieces of what we assumed to be dried meats hanging from the deckheads, which to us were definitely 'on the nose', together with eggs of various hues buried in what appeared to be compost in cardboard boxes.

Fortunately for me on most occasions, any knowledge of the species or part of the animal, fish or bird, from which a meal had been prepared did not impair my enjoyment, the actual taste being my main criterion. Hoping to alleviate a brother officer's apprehension of the forthcoming meal who liked mature cheese, Gorgonzola, etc, I suggested to him, if blindfolded, after smelling them, would he eat them?

However, the meal generally was a success, but it obviously required, by some, strong willpower to eat but with a false sense of enjoyment. For my part, after enjoying a portion of very tender and tasty meat, I jokingly said to the steward 'That was a nice piece of cat'. He replied 'No sir, it was a very special bit of doggee'. I didn't bother to ask him from which part of man's best friend - my enthusiasm had waned!

Pottinger Street viewed from Queen's Road. Central C1946
(Hong Kong information Services photograph)

Chapter Eighteen

HOMEWARD BOUND

IT was during December 1946 that we learned that our sea transport office duties in the Indonesian area were no longer required and that we would be returning to the UK. What wonderful news, after tramping in those beautiful but steaming islands for so long.

Our homeward voyage was, however, going to be the long way round, eastwards from Singapore to Vancouver and through the Panama Canal. It would be months before we arrived home - but we accepted the news with stoicism, an attitude we had learnt from our Chinese crew.

The voyage was to be 'light ship' and fuel oil was still carefully rationed. Consequently the STO's allocation for Liberty ships was the minimum for the distance, allowing only a small tonnage in hand to cater for unforeseen circumstances. Despite this, Captain Williams insisted on an additional 500 tons and we and the ship were later to benefit from his experience and determination to obtain additional fuel.

Soon after leaving Singapore the weather in the North Pacific deteriorated and during the latter part of the voyage we experienced days of storms which made our passage 'light ship' very precarious indeed. Even at reduced speed (about six knots) the propeller was out of the water more than it was in and rough seas pounded the ship mercilessly with the racing propeller's re-entry vibrations adding to the creaking, straining hull's stresses.

Every effort was made by the watch-keeping engineers to anticipate the moment when the propeller became airborne and closing the flap/throttle valve before the inertia governor slammed it shut, in order to minimise the main engine racing. This action greatly reduced the shock torque on the tail-end when the propeller smashed into the sea again. There were many watches under these conditions when an engineer had to be 'on the throttle' throughout the watch - a physically tiring duty so that sleep was very welcome in one's bunk, provided you could wedge yourself in to stop being pitched out!

Moving around the engine room was hazardous and in the stokehold the engineer had to acquire a real skill in being able to estimate the water level in the boiler drums when it was constantly moving with the roll of the ship, from 'no water' to 'full glass'. I was always filled with wonderment as to how the finely adjusted engine and complicated auxiliaries continued to function satisfactorily when being subjected to such violent movement and distortion of their supporting structures. Also when major surges of water in the boiler drums failed to cause priming (water mixed with steam) which could have caused damage to the machinery. Never before or since have I seen a tail-end shaft and stern tube take such a hammering. It was no surprise to learn when we arrived at Vancouver, that a number of Liberty ships had lost their propellers under similar weather conditions.

At sea, March 1946, left to right, SWS, Mr Plant fifth engineer, Mr Tipping third engineer and Mr Ridley fourth engineer

Another interesting feature of our voyage was how we and our resident insect population was affected by the change from tropical to winter weather in the North Pacific, after spending 19 months in and around the equatorial zones of the Indian and Pacific Oceans.

We Europeans had eventually become acclimatised to the hot humid weather, after bouts of ringworm, dhobi-itch, prickly heat, athlete's foot and found that if one broke the skin the blood was watery and did not clot easily. The ringworm was tackled with copious quantities of gentian violet and the athlete's foot kept at bay by keeping the feet clean and dry with plenty of talcum powder. The wooden duckboards were later removed, since it was discovered that they harboured the fungi. However, we were lucky in managing to avoid the dreaded 'lurgy' Tic Douloureux!

Our Chinese crew were completely at home; as far as I can remember they required no medical treatment. However, we did have two crew members who were registered opium addicts and I believe were allowed a bona fide allowance of opium. When inspecting the steering gear on an evening watch, I stumbled upon one of them in the process of enjoying a pipe, the obnoxious smell has been imprinted in my mind to this day.

The ship itself was also infested, presumably because of the long spells in harbour, the hull had become covered with marine growth which formed long green tentacles. Our short two to three-day trips did not reveal the extent to which this condition had reduced the *Samtay*'s speed, but eventually a longer voyage made it apparent. Moans from Captain Williams resulted in a meticulous examination of the engine room machinery to ensure maximum efficiency, but it showed no improvement. However, a short spell in brackish water, up river, near Bangkok killed some of the growth and improved the ship's speed by half a knot. Proving beyond doubt that fouling was to blame and no further improvement could be made until the ship was dry-docked for hull cleaning.

As we sailed into cooler waters we found the warmer parts of our accommodation being invaded by all sorts of creepy crawlies. When Monty Wright, the second mate, invited us to look in Nos 4 and 5 holds, where the propeller shaft tunnel passed through, we saw an amazing sight; the tops and sides of the tunnel were alive with layers of insect stowaways, three to six inches deep, all striving to commandeer the warm metal surfaces. It was their last refuge in the vast empty cold holds. Eventually, before we reached Vancouver the insects died and buckets of their bodies committed to the deep which would have been thought wasteful by some peoples in the tropics who consider them nutritious and even a delicacy.

Everyone felt the change to cold weather after so long in the tropics, but our Chinese crew suffered most of all. Their faces seemed to shrivel and became a deeper shade of yellow. Furthermore, they had no warm clothing, discarded potato sacks were tailored Shanghai-fashion (someway removed from Saville Row!) to keep out the cold when scurrying to carry out their duties outside the accommodation. My engine room crowd were lucky compared with their deck colleagues. Our own civilian wardrobe was sparse, having used our clothing coupons for uniforms, etc, and somewhat dilapidated in pre-War styles.

Arrival in Vancouver produced a transformation to the *Samtay*'s crew. At first we wondered who all the well-dressed gentlemen could be coming aboard after the first night in port. The elegant and expensive overcoats, hats and warm clothing, etc. so transformed our men so that we hardly recognised them - a genuine case of sackcloth to riches! Indeed, it was a little embarrassing when on occasions we met them afterwards, leaving or returning to the ship. We must have appeared to be the poorer crew members by observers.

From Vancouver the spare accommodation was occupied by a lady passenger with two teenage daughters returning to the UK.

At last we were on our final leg homewards. The unmarried officers were hoping the *Samtay* would not arrive before 5 April, as this would result in a tax bonus for them. At that time a single man could claim income tax rebate for time spent outside the UK after the first fiscal year, when married men had to be away two years. So a financial orientated voyage started when we left New Westminster and Victoria BC via the Panama Canal to Curacao for fuel. Our married colleagues growled their displeasure on the unfairness of we 'freelancers' being given a monetary advantage by not taking on marital responsibilities. I must confess it was the only time my engineering professionalism was subjected to temptation to economise on fuel and with the 'singles' hoping for bad weather to retard our progress.

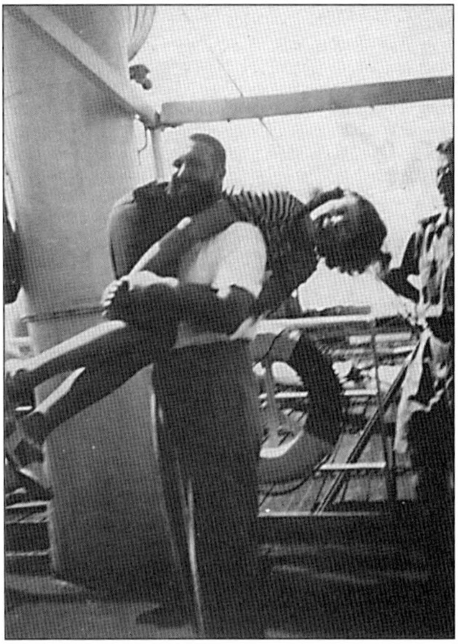

'Jimmy the One' back to normal (who lost his beard in Chapter 15) gives a lift to one of our teenage passengers, with me keeping a weather eye on him! Note the for'd deck stacked with timber.

If we had arrived home on 20 April 1947 the *Samtay* would have been away since May 1945, one year and eleven months. But she had nothing to gain whenever she arrived, she trundled her way homewards, with a very dirty bottom, fully loaded in appearance, because there was a 10–15-foot stack of timber on deck making a continuous platform from boat deck to poop. But no way did she loiter, she had the bit in her teeth and romped home on the 30 March 1947 – five days too soon for the 'singles'.

We were greeted by Mr Blachford, our superintendent, in a businesslike manner. 'I see, Mr Swain, that you have your chief's diesel time in. Good, we have a new passenger cargo ship building in Cammell Laird's, Birkenhead, for you. Have a nice long leave and please stand by her building. You can have a day off to get your chief's endorsement, it will be necessary because she will have main steam turbines and diesel generators with all-electric auxiliaries, Good luck.' My next three years' service had been settled in ten minutes flat!

That one day off was all I did get, Mr McLean, our Liverpool superintendent saw to that, but he was fondly remembered, being a large 'heavy steaming' bluff Scotsman who wielded the largest black fountain pen one had ever seen.

It transpired later that my new ship would be the *Brasil Star*, a fine and happy ship, which provided some social interest meeting passengers, whilst maintaining a regular schedule to South America and Brazil with her three sister ships, *Argentina Star*, *Uruguay Star* and *Paraguay Star*.

Brasil Star

Picture of engine room staff off duty, including doctor, voyage 4 homeward bound, 6 August 1948, (three engineers on watch).

Left to right: Mr Alexander, assistant engineer; Mr Walsham, chief refrig; SWS, second engineer; Mr Fraser, second electrician; Dr Gibbons; Mr Waugh, senior third engineer; Mr MacGarry, second refrig; Mr White, fourth engineer; Mr Henson, assistant engineer; Mr Pearcy, chief electrician; Mr Hocking, assistant engineer and Mr Ward, chief engineer.

Chapter Nineteen

THE LONG HAULS

VOYAGES at sea were more acceptable when one could see a changing landscape or passage through islands, but the time in port gave a real relief to monotonous shipboard routine. In many ports where cargo discharge or loading was of short duration and watch-keeping maintained, the few hours spent ashore were relaxing therapy. Change in scenery, company and first-time visits provided a fund of interest for all tastes which proved an education in itself. First-hand experience in foreign lands, although limited in time and usually restricted to coastal towns or ports, gave a sound basis on which to build one's knowledge and understanding of other countries' cultures.

During the War years many voyages were extended at anchor awaiting convoy assembly, passages lengthened by indirect routes (on a zig-zag course) and convoys' speed often governed by the slowest ship, sometimes half the capability of the majority. However, on reflection I think the pre-War long hauls from Australia to the UK were the most soul destroying. One can say the voyages during the War were never dull, very often in company with other ships and the most unwelcome attention of enemy, air, surface and under-water craft/vessels!

Leaving Melbourne pre-War homeward bound, to me was no pleasure, knowing that a 30-day non-stop passage lay ahead with no sight of land and then just a few hours at anchor at St Vincent taking on water and sufficient fuel to sail to the UK and a return voyage to the Cape Verde Isles. The 60-odd, 4-hour watches on the main or in my case (on the *Australia Star*) 30 8-hour spells of duty on the freezer were no problem and passed quickly; it was the hours in between after horizontal 'bunk exercise' had been completed. I must admit many a free hour was spent studying for my ticket, perhaps a bonus in disguise.

However, there were compensations, provided one were naturally attuned to observe the sometimes spectacular phenomena taking place around the ship in her isolation with the elements. It was my first voyage, after leaving Melbourne, September 1938, which provided a spectacularly rough passage all the way, leaving the Bass Straight, across the Indian Ocean and some days after rounding the Cape of Good Hope (no sight of land). Understandably, Great Circle sailing took us well south and for days we ploughed our way through very cold stormy seas.

To me with only 18-months' sea-time, the pounding the *Australia Star* took under slightly reduced engine power was frightening. One moved about the ship with difficulty and in the mid-ships accommodation, hearing the speed of the main diesels change to slow heavy groaning as the stern sank deep and the bow became airborne, was impressive. In seconds the bow plunged deeply into the next wave to a quickening engine speed causing a terrific crash, the whole ship vibrating while the propellers bit into the sea with engine revs falling until their power moved the ship forward again, the accommodation creaking continuously as it altered to its changing shape. On one occasion I literally saw a new crack appear in the linoleum under my feet but when it was pointed out to a senior engineer, he assured me 'that the time to worry was when this did not happen, it shows the "old girl" is flexing nicely and thereby spreading the shock forces'. It took me some time to understand and appreciate that fact.

Australia Star *on right, at Port Melbourne loading for the long haul*

Most of the refrigerated spaces were monitored from the frig. engine room with electrical thermometers, but Nos 1 and 6 holds had to be checked by hand thermometers. These were suspended on cords attached to removable brass caps on the main deck. During rough weather it was dangerous to use this facility, so until conditions improved, we were able to monitor the spaces by checking the temperature of the refrigerant (brine) returns in the engine room.

The operating conditions of a diesel engine could be checked by the condition of the exhaust. On the *Australia Star* provision had been made to climb up inside the funnel for this purpose. It was during rough weather when I made a visit to the top of the funnel, whilst holding on with both hands, that I was given a sea-bird's eye view of the ship battling against the elements. It was awe-inspiring. Looking for'd seeing the gyrating main mast following the fo'c's'le head disappear into a huge wave accompanied by a change in beat of the main engines and then the deluge of sea-water flooding the well-deck with heavy spray whipping over the bridge and funnel. Conditions aft showed less deck flooding but the vibrations caused by the pounding seas were added to by the racing propellers.

I was transfixed for a long time watching the changing scene as the ship fought the wind and the seas, until my attention was attracted to a flight of albatross hovering effortlessly, a few feet above my head on each side of the funnel. They had been accompanying the ship for days appearing a few hours after day-break, disappearing before dusk. The larger ones would glide quite close to me looking down with their black eyes and then with an indiscernible change in wing attitude, move forward as if the ship were stationary, then planing down towards the stern, ever ready to swoop down after any garbage tossed into the ship's wake. One could not help but admire how these wonderful birds used the elements to transport themselves over hundreds of miles of sea with a minimum expended energy. Little did I realise at the time how a certain Mr Mitchell, the designer of the Spitfire, in the not too distant future, by similar observations, would incorporate characteristics of the seabirds' wings into his design which improved the performance of the Spitfires enabling it to out-manoeuvre German fighter planes.

View from the funnel

View from fore-deck

There is no doubt that the accompanying albatross provided an interest in the passage across the unrelenting, inhospitable Indian Ocean. We were able to recognise some by their individual markings and they were given names like Black Jack and Flighty Matilda. When some days after rounding The Cape our squadron of albatross disappeared, they were greatly missed. Indeed one can understand why seafarers respect these wonderful birds and consider it an ill omen when one is killed by man.

As the ship progressed northwards towards the Equator the warmer weather and smoother passage made a welcome change but the rising sea and air temperatures meant that the refrigeration department was entering its most demanding time. All refrigeration spaces were well insulated but their disposition in the ship was inevitably affected by adjacent spaces, eg, frozen meat in a lower hold could lower the temperature of a cheese deck above. This point was taken into consideration in the loading plan when the characteristics and previous voyage records were known. The wide range of temperatures required for the safe carriage of frozen meat and butter to the higher levels for apples, cheese, eggs and wine made the placing of the different foods in the vessel important. In addition to these variants, the daily change in sea and air temperatures and the need to vent the fruit spaces to keep an acceptable level of carbon dioxide, made the chief refrigeration engineer's responsibility a demanding one. This was recognised by the Blue Star Line because he was always considered to be next in rank to the chief engineer.

We already thought that some of the eggs in a deck below casks of wine would be stained because during the rough weather it had been reported that trickles of wine had been seen in the tunnel bilges. Unloading in London showed this to be true when many cases of red eggs were discharged with the inevitable reduction in market value, although one wondered if the lacing by red wine would have improved their taste!

Already the Brush diesels were operating at full power as we neared the Equator, while the main engines and electrical generators running with a steady beat were accompanied by the drone of the ventilating fans blowing fresh air down into the engine rooms and accommodation areas. On smooth seas the ship maintained a constant speed of 17–18 knots, using her 2,465 hp, helping to make up for some of the lost time during the rough weather and leaving a straight wake astern as far as the eye could see. The only movements one could see were the small flying fish flitting away from the bow-waves as they spread in ever widening Vs.

On the freezer careful adjustments were made to brine flows in the main and for'd brine rooms in order to maintain the required temperatures in the food spaces within the limited capacity of the refrigeration plant. Some of the apple decks' carbon dioxide levels required reduction, so regular checks on deck were made with a whirling hydrometer (wet and dry thermometers on a frame like a rattle), to assess humidity levels. In conjunction with weather forecasts and estimated ship's position, a day would be selected when humidity would be at a minimum. Then the spaces would be vented until the CO_2 levels were satisfactory, thereby keeping the frosting of the cold air batteries to a minimum.

Another problem on some of the hand thermometer positions, was the build up of ice caused by a leaking deck cap or condensation where the pipe passed through a shelter deck at normal air temperature. The ice formed a collar which prevented withdrawal of the suspended thermometer to take a reading. Various methods were used to cut away the obstruction sometimes many feet down the tube. Dumpers were the most successful, steel rods with a serrated head, were repeatedly dropped onto the ice until a breakthrough was made. The success rate depended on the depth of formed ice.

Repeated efforts to clear one position had failed so I thought it worth trying a dumper suitably made red hot with a large blow-lamp. It was a completely black night, no moon or stars with a brisk wind. I used the for'd mast house to heat the dumper and then proceeded along the deck with it at arms-length on a wire, lowering it into the thermometer tube. It proved successful. At breakfast later, the second mate told me what a scare I had given him, when he suddenly saw a glowing 'red thing' appear and creep out of the mast-house weaving about a foot above the deck, snaking its way for'd and then suddenly disappearing!

On this trip two decks of chilled beef, carried in an atmosphere of 9%-12% CO_2 had been undertaken to ascertain the practicability and economics of carrying fresh meat for five to six weeks. The shorter voyages, two weeks from the Argentine with no special arrangements other than a steady temperature of $29\frac{1}{2}°$ Fahrenheit, were most successful. Maintaining the level of CO_2 required regular attention which entailed injecting the gas into the space through the fire extinguisher points with thermometer deck caps removed; a time consuming task and involved the replacing of dozens of heavy steel bottles, a laborious job which had to be carried out with care on a moving ship. Most of the topping up was allocated to my watch, the midnight-8. The meat was unloaded in London in prime condition but I believe the extra costs involved made it too expensive.

It was a relief when we reached Tenerife and the few hours spent taking on water and fuel, provided a change seeing land and watching the small nude boys diving for pennies but we were soon under way again on the last leg of our voyage.

Left St Vincent, Tenerife

Below: Small boys diving for pennies

Looking back on those long voyages, as a young man, they were monotonous and to some extent boring but today I am sure they have contributed towards my appreciating some of the real wonders in life.

On the one hand, experiencing the unbelievable way the mass of complicated machinery, working to tolerances of a thousandth part of an inch, continued to function reliably day after day in a structure which was flexing violently in all directions. An engineering accolade. But on the other hand, how nature designs and provides the fish in the sea and the bird life above to function perfectly and efficiently in all seasons, with a minimum of effort.

Chapter Twenty

GUARDIAN ANGEL(S)

ON reflection I now know that on two occasions during my 12 years at sea there must have been a guardian angel poised above my head saving me from serious injury or body disfigurement with only seconds to spare.

Angels

The first incident occurred during my fourth voyage on the *Stuart Star* (December 1937) after only seven months sea service, and the second during July 1944 in Madras when serving in the *Samtay* seven years later.

Coal firing the *Stuart*'s boilers was one of my early challenges in which I realised that the only way to obtain a satisfactory steam output was to be able to understand the men's characters and 'lead from the front'. This meant that I must be able to physically fire the boilers as well as they could, or better. This decision was reached during the early part of the outward bound voyage to Australia via South Africa and by the time Cape Town was reached I was able to run a fairly efficient team in the stokehold.

My physical attributes needed for firing had been progressively developed and were no problem but understanding the men's outlook was much more difficult. I am sure that the coal-fired stokehold in the *Stuart* and similar ships I served in later provided an excellent training ground for the study of human psychology and an insight into managing men.

The four boilers, two single-ended and two double-ended, had four fires at each end tended by one fireman. The rate of steaming was measured by the engineer officer by the amount of feed water returned to each boiler. The single-ended boilers presented no difficulty but the double-ended having a fireman at each end, made it impossible to ascertain when the rate of steaming was reduced, which fireman's effort was below normal - who was swinging the lead.

After leaving Cape Town I strongly suspected that one fireman was not pulling his weight on a double ended boiler, and he insinuated surreptitiously that it was the other man who was slacking. I told him I would take over on the next raking sequence, but contrary to what he expected, I took over his end of the boiler. I was not surprised when I found he was carrying 'bright fronts', that is a roaring fire just inside the furnace with the remaining five feet of the furnace empty of burning coal. There was no need for me to comment, his bluff had been called and shown up before the rest of the firemen - a serious situation in any coal-firing team.

Later on, when I returned to the stokehold after executing engine room duties, I suddenly saw my 'found out fireman' advancing towards me out of the smoke and gloom of the stokehold with a red-hot iron rake in his hands. I was rooted to the spot with fear knowing that his intention was to brand my chest with the rake.

My guardian angel must have intervened because when the rake was within inches of my chest (I could feel the heat through my boilersuit), he dropped the rake with a clatter on the floorplates and burst into tears. The tension in the stokehold was electric. I retreated to the engine room to recover my composure.

There was no further problem with the fireman but I decided not to report him for his serious breach of discipline which may have proved beneficial later. At Port Elizabeth when a colleague and myself entered a pub for a drink, there at the other end of the bar was my culprit with two of his cronies. I warned my companion that there may be trouble from that quarter and urged him to drink up so we could retire as quickly as possible. We were in the process of downing our drinks, when swishing along the bar came two pints of beer with the compliments of my fireman. We drank their health with a sigh of relief and made a thankful departure.

The second occasion was about six years later when serving in the *Samtay*. Again it was the behaviour of a fireman on my watch who turned out to be a man with a schizophrenic personality. During his watch-keeping duties he was a likeable young man carrying out his work conscientiously and having an artistic talent of being able to draw caricatures of our crew members, which proved to be very lifelike.

The darker side of his personality soon became apparent when he had been drinking alcohol which made him completely unmanageable and fierce. The first time his split personality appeared was in Port Said when he was returned to the ship by the police in a near uncontrollable condition. Later, disciplinary action had to be taken by the skipper and at the time I pleaded that his behaviour during his watch keeping duties, so far, had been completely satisfactory and urged this factor to be taken into consideration. After the 'logging' I talked to my fireman like a Dutch uncle stressing the point that at all times he must abstain completely from any form of alcohol. I included, in the interview a greaser (who claimed to be a relative and who accompanied him ashore), emphasising the need for complete abstinence. He promised to help.

My fireman's behaviour was satisfactory during the next port of call at Colombo where shore leave was granted. However, at the next, Madras, Mr Reid and I had just finished our light supper about 10.00pm, when we saw a figure staggering towards the ship's gangway. It was dark but I thought I recognised the man to be my fireman and we were both concerned with what we had seen.

Anyway, we turned in and I had just put out my bunk light, when a terrific commotion occurred in the accommodation below our deck, I looked out into our alleyway, which was only lit with small wattage blue lights (part of the War-time blackout), when suddenly a figure rushed past me whom I recognised to be our chief steward - he was running for his life. To my horror rushing towards me brandishing an axe above his head was my fireman. There was no escape, I just froze in the narrow alleyway.

My guardian angel saved me again, because when he was within a foot of me the madman recognised me, lowered the axe and burst into tears. I spoke to him gently by name asking for the axe which he gave to me and I thankfully passed it on to Mr Reid who had just arrived behind me. Members of the crew who had been following in his wake, forcibly removed him, because he had become violent again and led him away to the hospital on the poop deck where he was put in a straight jacket till morning. In the meantime a search was made for our chief steward who was eventually found on the 'monkey island' above the bridge. The poor man had had a terrible experience. It transpired that my fireman had demanded him to open the beer locker and supply him with drink, and when refused, had returned to the chief steward's cabin with an axe. Fortunately he had managed to evade him and escaped at speed from the lower deck.

All Liberty ships carried axes clipped to the bulkheads and distributed throughout the accommodation so that external doors could be smashed down to enable occupants to escape if they became jammed, due to structural distortion, which often occurred after enemy action from bombs or torpedoes. There were also knock-out panels in all cabin doors.

It was obvious after this incident that it would have been unsafe to allow the fireman to continue with his shipboard duties, so he was discharged into the custody of the hospital authorities in Madras.

The *Samtay* returned to England and on our third voyage we again returned to India and called at Madras some months later. To our surprise the shipping agent brought aboard a small suitcase containing the pitiful belongings of our fireman. Apparently sometime after we left Madras he absconded from the hospital and no trace of him had since been found.

On our return to the UK Captain Williams had the sorrowful task of handing the man's belongings to the authorities to be sent to his next of kin in Glasgow.

Chapter Twenty One

POSTSCRIPT TO THE LAST VOYAGE OF THE *STUART STAR*

DURING latter years my wife and I have been fortunate to have been able to visit some of my old stamping grounds: Australia, New Zealand, Canada and the West Coast of the USA.

It was while we were walking the decks of the *Queen Mary* at Long Beach, California, that I recalled vivid memories of the week in December 1943 when she carried thousands of servicemen and women to New York. Among them were two complete Blue Star Line crews destined to man two Liberty ships. Again, when we were in the first-class lounge on the *Mary* which was, I think, during the War used for the officers' lounge, I could picture the scene - hundreds of Allied officers painfully drinking lemonade, Coca-Cola, etc, - a depressing sight! But not for the handful of service women who had the potential attention of all those men, including Douglas Fairbanks, Junior, the film star who was then serving in the United States Navy.

The *Queen Mary* was a 'dry' ship when she carried Allied forces. It helped to curb the over exuberance of the 'passengers' which could occur between nationals during their stay in confined, overcrowded, accommodation on board ship. I was lucky, by a remarkable coincidence, while I was walking on the boat deck, on the fourth day out, a young officer on a deck above called me by name. To my surprise I recognised he was a man from the same firm I had served my apprenticeship! He had approached me several times during my visits to the works when on leave, being keen to follow in my footsteps. This he had done, so we were able to celebrate in his cabin with 'real' drinks, his achievement in becoming an assistant engineer on the *Queen Mary*. We have never met since.

It was after Christmas that we took over the Liberty ships, the *ss Samnid* and *ss Samtay*, the latter being my ship. She was assembled in 26 days at the Bethlehem Fairfield Shipyard, Inc, Baltimore, Maryland, USA. We understood that the average assembly time of these British designed ships was 14 days, but the *Samtay* had taken a little longer (26 days) because of the winter weather, way below freezing I recall, and the beginning of the Christmas holiday.

In 1985 Mrs Swain and I contemplated making a carpetbaggers' tour of South Africa. I wrote to newspapers in East London and Port Elizabeth in April to ascertain whether, during our visit, their archives would be available for me to extract copies of the *Stuart Star* incident. I received favourable replies, but one from a Mr Ross enclosed a copy of an article from the *Port Elizabeth Post*, 21 June 1985, giving a full resumé on the wreck of the *Stuart*. The article had been instigated from numerous enquiries being made as to the identity of parts of an old wreck at Hood Point. It was interesting to know that parts of the *Stuart* were still there!

Unfortunately, in October of that year, because of the media reports on South Africa continued to indicate a deteriorating racial condition, we ruefully postponed our trip.

However, during November 1987 my wife and I were able to spend a very interesting and enjoyable holiday in South Africa. Wc had a week in Cape Town exploring the wine-growing areas and the Cape of Good Hope, after which we joined a coach touring the Garden Route, terminating at Durban. The over-night stops included one at East London.

When staying at the Beach Island Hotel, Plettenburg Bay, we met a Mr and Mrs Poynton. Mr Poynton remembered the *Stuart* wreck when he was a small boy at Port Elizabeth, and because our schedule made it impossible to visit the newspaper offices during normal office hours, he kindly volunteered to visit them on our behalf when they returned from their holiday.

We continued our very pleasant tour, beautiful weather, etc, but at Grahamstown two days later it became overcast and rained all the way to East London. Furthermore, we fell behind schedule, consequently reaching East London one and a half hours late! It was prematurely dark and when travelling along the coast towards the town, I noted that the visibility was nearly as bad as it was 50 years ago! - was this an omen? Consequently our planned dash in a taxi to Hood Point had to be aborted, much to my disappointment, and an early morning start to travel to Umtata in the Transkei prevented the opportunity to go there before we left.

Epilogue 1988

Two days before my visit to Mr Tune, Blue Star Line's chief superintendent, in May 1988, low and behold, a letter from Mr and Mrs Poynton arrived (six months after seeing them in Plettenburg Bay) with photostat copies of the *Eastern Herald*, dated 18 and 20 December 1937, with a picture and full details of the wreck story! I was overjoyed at receiving them and shall always be indebted to them for their valiant effort. I erroneously gave them the 13 November when it should have been the 17 and this, coupled with the care with which the old newspapers had to be handled by the reference library staff under strict surveillance, accounted for the delays. Furthermore, the papers were not to be moved because of their fragility, so Mr Poynton had to get a photographer to take pictures of the relevant articles.

My brief meeting with Mr Tune was very enjoyable and his gift of a copy of *Blue Star* by Tony Atkinson and Kevin O'Donoghue was much appreciated and made fascinating reading. If it were possible, what stories those ships could tell of their time afloat and the experiences of the people who sailed in them.

It was with sadness that I read that all the ten ships I sailed in had now gone: three torpedoed during the War: *ss Avelona Star*; *mv Imperial Star* (the trip after I left her!) and *ss Royal Star*. Six broken up: *mv Australia Star*; *ss Fresno Star*; *mv Sydney Star*; *ss Empire Might*; *ss Samtay* and *ss Brasil Star*. But parts of the *Stuart Star* survived.

My wife who has helped me with the composition and writing of the stories, thinks I am over sensitive - all this fuss over a few tons of scrap-iron! But I wonder really if she is a wee bit jealous of the *Stuart Star*, my first sea-going girl friend, figuratively speaking, who still attracts me to that rocky shore in the southern hemisphere!

Glossary of Terms

B-ol'man on backend: An accumulation of slag/clinker which sometimes formed at the innermost end of the fire-grate, usually caused by not properly removing all clinker when fires were cleaned.

Bulkhead dynamo: An oil lamp - a relic from the times when the harbour boiler was shut down and banked for the night to save coal.

Fiddley: A series of iron grating connected with ladders to give access to for'd and aft stokeholds from deck level.

Field-days: Extra work to the two four-hour watch-keeping duties but with no extra salary! Usually five two-hour spells every two weeks repairing and maintaining the steam winches on deck or any work that the second engineer deemed necessary.

Jumbo: A similar tool to the slice but much heavier, sometimes requiring two men to lift into a high fire box. Used to break up clinker formed on the fire-bars and to remove any B-ol'man on backend.

Monkey island: A small bridge with binnacle above the wheelhouse.

On the blood: Maintaining the steam pressure just below the red line on the boiler pressure gauge above which the safety valves would lift - a loss of energy and precious fresh water - an act of incompetence!

On the rattle: In order to keep the activities of the firemen on each boiler in unison, the leading fireman would vigorously rattle his shovel on the bulkhead or any metal nearby, making a signal to commence firing, slicing, etc.

Peggy: Rating whose duties were to clean their watch's accommodation, carry food from galley midships to the poop in all weathers - a steward's duty for the watch.

Slice: A heavy poker 8 to 10 feet long with a flat chisel-shaped end which was forced into the fire at fire-bar level to lift the burning coal, thus allowing air to pass through to improve combustion.